KETO
AIR FRYER

How To Make Delightful Yet Low Carb, Low Fat, and Low Cholesterol Meat and Vegetable Dishes For The Whole Family

CORDELL WARNER

Copyright © 2020 Cordell Warner

All Rights Reserved

Copyright 2020 By Cordell Warner - All rights reserved.

The following book is produced below with the goal of providing information that is as accurate and reliable as possible. Regardless, purchasing this eBook can be seen as consent to the fact that both the publisher and the author of this book are in no way experts on the topics discussed within and that any recommendations or suggestions that are made herein are for entertainment purposes only. Professionals should be consulted as needed prior to undertaking any of the action endorsed herein.

This declaration is deemed fair and valid by both the American Bar Association and the Committee of Publishers Association and is legally binding throughout the United States.

Furthermore, the transmission, duplication or reproduction of any of the following work including specific information will be considered an illegal act irrespective of if it is done electronically or in print. This extends to creating a secondary or tertiary copy of the work or a recorded copy and is only allowed with express written consent from the Publisher. All additional right reserved.

The information in the following pages is broadly considered to be a truthful and accurate account of facts and as such any inattention, use or misuse of the information in question by the reader will render any resulting actions solely under their purview. There are no scenarios in which the publisher or the original author of this work can be in any fashion deemed liable for any hardship or damages that may befall them after undertaking information described herein.

Additionally, the information in the following pages is intended only for informational purposes and should thus be thought of as universal. As befitting its nature, it is presented without assurance regarding its prolonged validity or interim quality. Trademarks that are mentioned are done without written consent and can in no way be considered an endorsement from the trademark holder.

Table of Contents

PART I 12

Keto Recipes 13

   Chapter 1: Gourmet Recipes 15

      Creamy Garlic Chicken 15

      Mediterranean Lemon Herb Chicken Salad 17

      Garlic Butter Scallops and Steak 20

      Fried Chicken 22

      Lime Chile Steak Fajitas 24

      Spaghetti Squash With Stuffed Lasagna 27

      Zucchini Boats With Stuffed Tuna 29

      Spinach and Goat Cheese Stuffed Breast of Chicken 31

   Chapter 2: Quick and Easy Recipes 33

      Antipasto Salad 33

      Feta Cheese and Chicken Plate 35

      Cheese Omelet 36

      Baked Salmon and Pesto 37

      Pork Chops and Blue Cheese Sauce 39

      Green Pepper and Pork Stir-Fry 41

      Broccoli With Fried Chicken 43

      Fried Eggs With Pork and Kale 44

   Chapter 3: Sweet Recipes 45

      Sugar Cinnamon Donuts 45

      Mug Brownie 47

      Mini Cheesecake 49

- Keto Fudge 52
- Peanut Butter Hearts 53
- Peanut Butter and White Chocolate Blondies 54
- Low Carb Ice Cream 55
- Chocolate Donut 57

Chapter 4: Savory Recipes 59
- Keto McMuffin 59
- Sausage Hash With Rainbow Chard 61
- Veggie and Chicken Sausage Skillet 63
- Cheese and Crispy Salami 64
- Buffalo Chicken Sandwich 65
- Cream Cheese and Salmon Bites 67
- Turkey Patties 70

Chapter 5: Poultry and Meat Recipes 71
- Beef Cabbage Skillet 71
- Meatball Casserole 73
- Beef Taquitos 75
- Chicken Wings 77
- Roasted Leg of Chicken 79

Chapter 6: Staple Recipes 82
- Keto Waffles 82
- Cookie Dough 84
- Baked Tofu 85
- Cauliflower Fried Rice 86

PART II 87

Air Fryer Recipes 88

Chapter 1: Chicken And Pork Recipes 90

Maple Chicken Thighs 90

Buttermilk Chicken 92

Cheddar-Stuffed BBQ Breasts of Chicken 94

Buffalo Chicken 96

Breaded Pork Chops 97

Pork Meatballs 99

Pork Jerky 99

Pork Skewers 101

Pork Tenderloin With Mustard Crust 104

Chapter 2: Beef And Fish Recipes 106

Beef Tenderloin 106

Beef Wontons 108

Mushrooms and Steak 110

Rib Eye Steak 111

Meatloaf 113

Fish Sticks 115

Cajun Salmon 117

Salmon Cakes and Sriracha Mayo 118

Cod With Sesame Crust and Snap Peas 120

Grilled Fish and Pesto Sauce 121

Chapter 3: Vegetarian Party Recipes 122

Apple Pies 122

Fruit Crumble 124

Kiwi Chips 125

Apple Crisp 126

Roasted Veggies 128

Eggplant Parmesan 131

French Fries 133

Sweet and Spicy Carrots 135

Baked Potatoes 136

Chapter 4: Vegetarian Appetizer Recipes 137

Crunchy Brussels Sprouts 137

Buffalo Cauliflower 138

Stuffed Mushrooms 140

Sweet Potatoes With Baked Taquitos 142

Cauliflower Curry 144

Air-Fried Avocado Wedges 145

Crunchy Grains 146

Buffalo Chickpeas 147

Easy Falafel 148

Mini Cheese and Bean Tacos 150

Green Beans and Spicy Sauce 152

Cheesy Sugar Snap Peas 154

PART III 155

Vegan Cookbook 156

Chapter 1: Breakfast Recipes 159

Shamrock Sandwich 159

Breakfast Burrito 161

Gingerbread Waffles 164

Green Chickpeas And Toast 166

Asparagus And Tomato Quiche 168

Breakfast Bowl 170

Tofu Pancakes 172

Chapter 2: Side Dish Recipes 174

Baked Beans 174

  Baked Potato Wedges 176

  Black Beans And Quinoa 177

  Roasted Lemon Garlic Broccoli 178

  Spicy Tofu 179

  Spanish Rice 181

  Pepper And Lemon Pasta 182

Chapter 3: High Protein Recipes 183

  Kale Salad With Spicy Tempeh Bits And Chickpeas 183

  Protein Bars 186

  Tofu And Spinach Scramble 188

  Vegan Tacos 189

  Grilled Tofu Steaks And Spinach Salad 191

  Corn, Quinoa, And Edamame Salad 194

  Lentil Soup 195

Chapter 4: Dessert Recipes 197

  Chocolate Pudding 197

  Orange Cake 199

  Pumpkin Tofu Pie 201

  Vegan Brownie 203

  Vegan Cupcake 204

  Vanilla Cake 206

  Miracle Fudge 208

Chapter 5: Sauces & Dips Recipes 210

  Tomato Jam 210

  Walnut Kale Pesto 211

  Ranch Dressing 212

PART III ... 214

Chapter 1: Introduction to the Heart-Healthy Diet ... 215

The Rules of the Heart-Healthy Diet ... 215

The Benefits of the Heart-Healthy Diet ... 216

Chapter 2: Heart-Healthy Savory Meals ... 218

Shrimp Scampi and Zoodles ... 218

Citrus Chicken Salad ... 219

Shrimp Taco Salad ... 221

Chicken, Green Bean, Bacon Pasta ... 222

Heart-Healthy "Fried" Chicken ... 224

Turkey Burgers and Slaw ... 225

Slow Cooked Shrimp and Pasta ... 227

Chapter 3: Heart-Healthy Sweet Treats ... 228

Chocolate Mousse ... 228

Baked Pears ... 229

Chocolate Peanut Butter Bites ... 230

Oatmeal Cookies ... 231

Pina Colada Frozen Dessert ... 232

Kiwi Sorbet ... 233

Ricotta Brûlée ... 234

Chapter 4: Heart-Healthy Gourmet Meals ... 235

Grilled Halibut With Pine Nut Relish ... 235

Shrimp Bowls ... 236

Grilled Watermelon Steak Salad ... 237

Crispy Cod and Green Beans ... 238

Pistachio-Crusted Fish ... 239

Cumin-Spiced Lamb and Salad 240

Chapter 5: Heart-Healthy Quick 'n Easy Meals 241

Sugar Snap Pea and Radish Salad 241

Horseradish Salmon Cakes 243

Salmon, Green Beans, and Tomatoes 244

Broccoli Pesto Fusilli 244

Strawberry Spinach Salad 246

One-Pot Shrimp and Spinach 247

Chapter 6: Heart-Healthy Vegetarian and Vegan Meals 248

Vegetarian Butternut Squash Torte 248

Vegetarian Fried Rice 249

Vegan Butternut Squash Soup 250

Vegetarian Kale and Sweet Potato Frittata 252

Vegan Ginger Ramen 254

Vegan Glazed Tofu 255

Vegan Greek Tofu Breakfast Scramble 256

PART I

Keto Recipes

The keto diet is a high-fat and low-carb diet that comes with various health benefits. It has been found that this diet can help you lose weight and improve the condition of your health. It might also show some positive effects on cancer, diabetes, Alzheimer's, and epilepsy. This diet's main aim is to reduce the intake of carbs drastically and replace the same with healthy fats. When you reduce the consumption of carbs, the body will enter a metabolic state known as ketosis. During ketosis, the body will try its best to burn the body fat for generating energy. It will also be turning the liver fat into ketones that supply energy to the brain.

A keto diet is a very effective way of losing weight. The best aspect of this diet is that you can lose bodyweight without counting calories. The reason behind this is that the diet will be so filling that you will not have frequent cravings. It has been found that people who follow a keto diet can lose 2.5 times more weight when compared to those people who follow a calorie-restrictive diet. The keto diet can also deal with type 2 diabetes, metabolic, and prediabetes syndrome. Some other benefits of the keto diet are:

- **Cancer:** This diet can help suppress the growth of tumors and might also help in treating various types of cancer.

- **Heart diseases:** The keto diet can help deal with various chronic heart conditions such as heart attack, stroke, and others.

- **Polycystic ovary:** This diet is well known for reducing insulin levels that can help in dealing with polycystic ovary.

There are certain food items that you will need to include while following this diet.

- **Fatty fish**: Trout, salmon, mackerel, tuna

- **Meat**: Steak, sausage, red meat, ham, chicken, bacon, turkey

- **Seeds and nuts**: Walnuts, almonds, pumpkin seeds, flax seeds, chia seeds

- **Oils**: Coconut oil, olive oil, avocado oil

A keto diet is an excellent option for all those who have diabetes, overweight or want to improve the health of their metabolism. I have included some tasty and easy keto recipes that you can include in your diet plan.

Chapter 1: Gourmet Recipes

If you are looking for some tasty keto gourmet recipes, this section has got what you are searching for. So, let's have a look at them.

Creamy Garlic Chicken

Total Prep & Cooking Time: Twenty-five minutes

Yields: Six servings

Nutrition Facts: Calories: 348 | Protein: 28g | Carbs: 6.3g | Fat: 22.3g | Fiber: 0.9g

Ingredients

- Two pounds of chicken breasts (sliced thinly)
- Two tbsps. of olive oil
- One cup of each
    - Heavy cream
    - Spinach (chopped)
- Half cup of each
    - Chicken stock
    - Parmesan cheese
    - Sun-dried tomatoes
- One tsp. of each
    - Italian seasoning
    - Garlic powder

Method:

1. Take an iron skillet and add olive oil in it. After the oil gets hot, add the chicken and cook for five minutes. Remove the pieces of chicken from the skillet. Keep aside.

2. Add chicken stock, heavy cream, Italian seasoning, garlic powder, and parmesan cheese in the skillet. Whisk the mixture on medium flame until the sauce thickens. Add tomatoes and spinach. Simmer the mixture for two minutes until the spinach wilts.

3. Addcooked chicken into the prepared sauce. Cook for two minutes.

4. Serve hot.

Mediterranean Lemon Herb Chicken Salad

Total Prep & Cooking Time: Twenty-five minutes

Yields: Four servings

Nutrition Facts: Calories: 326 | Protein: 22.3g | Carbs: 12g | Fat: 20.1g | Fiber: 6.2g

Ingredients

- Two tbsps. of each
    - Olive oil
    - Water
    - Parsley (chopped)
    - Red wine vinegar
    - Basil (dried)
    - Garlic (minced)
- One lemon (juiced)
- One tsp. of each
    - Salt
    - Oregano
- One pound of chicken thighs

For the salad:

- Four cups of lettuce leaves (washed)
- One cucumber (diced)
- Two tomatoes (diced)
- One onion (sliced)
- One avocado (sliced)
- One-third cup of kalamata olives (sliced)
- Wedges of lemon (for serving)

Method:

1. Whisk all the marinade ingredients in a bowl. Pour half of the marinade in a shallow dish. Store the remaining marinade for the dressing.

2. Add the pieces of chicken in the marinade dish and marinate for half an hour.

3. Mix all the ingredients for the salad in a mixing bowl and keep aside.

4. Heat some oil in a grill pan. Add the marinated chicken and cook for five minutes on each side until browned on all sides.

5. Slice the chicken pieces.

6. Serve the salad with chicken from the top. Drizzle some of the marinade and serve with lemon wedges.

Garlic Butter Scallops and Steak

Total Prep & Cooking Time: Thirty minutes

Yields: Two servings

Nutrition Facts: Calories: 280 | Protein: 23.1g | Carbs: 1.2g | Fat: 1.3g | Fiber: 0.3g

Ingredients

- Two fillets of beef tenderloin
- Black pepper and kosher salt (according to taste)
- Three tbsps. of butter
- Ten sea scallops

For the sauce:

- Three garlic cloves (minced)
- Six tbsps. of butter (cubed)
- Two tbsps. of each
    - Chives (chopped)
    - Parsley (chopped)
- One tbsp. of lemon juice
- Two tsps. of lemon zest

- Black pepper and kosher salt (according to taste)

Method:

1. Take an iron skillet and heat it over medium flame for ten minutes.

2. Season the steak with pepper and salt.

3. Add two tbsps. of butter in the skillet. Add the steak and cook for six minutes on each side. Cook until the steak reaches your desired doneness.

4. Keep the steak aside and heat one tbsp. of butter in the skillet.

5. Remove the muscles from the small side of the scallops and wash them with cold running water.

6. Season the scallops with pepper and salt. Cook the scallops on each side for three minutes.

7. For making the sauce, add garlic and butter in a skillet. Stir for one minute. Add chives, lemon zest, parsley, and lemon juice. Add pepper and salt for seasoning.

8. Serve the scallops and steak with butter sauce from the top.

Fried Chicken

Total Prep & Cooking Time: Fifty minutes

Yields: Twelve servings

Nutrition Facts: Calories: 305 | Protein: 38.2g | Carbs: 0.6g | Fat: 12.3g | Fiber: 0.5g

Ingredients

- Four ounces of pork rinds
- Two tsps. of thyme (dried)
- One tsp. of each

- Black pepper
- Salt
- Oregano (dried)
- Half tsp. of garlic powder
- One-third tsp. of paprika (smoked)
- Twelve chicken legs
- One large egg
- Two ounces of mayonnaise
- Three tbsps. of Dijon mustard

Method:

1. Crush the pork rinds for making powder texture. Leave some of the big pieces.

2. Preheat the oven at 200 degrees Celsius.

3. Mix salt, pork rinds, thyme, pepper, garlic powder, oregano, and paprika. Spread out the prepared mixture on a large flat dish.

4. Combine Dijon mustard, egg, and mayonnaise in a bowl. Dip the chicken legs in the egg mixture and then roll in the mixture of pork rind. Coat well.

5. Place the legs of chicken on a baking tray. Bake for forty minutes.

6. Serve hot.

Lime Chile Steak Fajitas

Total Prep & Cooking Time: Twenty-five minutes

Yields: Four servings

Nutrition Facts: Calories: 419 | Protein: 23.1g | Carbs: 12g | Fat: 25.6g | Fiber: 5.1g

Ingredients

For the marinade:

- Two tbsps. of olive oil
- One-third cup of lime juice
- Three tbsps. of cilantro (chopped)
- Two garlic cloves (chopped)
- One tsp. of brown sugar
- Three-fourth tsp. of chili flakes
- Half tsp. of cumin (ground)
- One tsp. of salt
- One pound of steak

For the fajitas:

- Three capsicums (different colors, sliced)
- One avocado (sliced)
- One onion (sliced)

For serving:

- Tortillas
- Sour cream

Method:

1. Combine all the marinade ingredients in a bowl. Keep aside half of the marinade. Pour the remaining marinade in a flat dish and marinate the steak.

2. Heat one tsp. of oil in a skillet. Add the steak and grill for five minutes on each side. Allow the steak to cool down for five minutes.

3. Wipe the skillet and brush some oil. Fry the capsicums along with the strips of onion. Add the reserved marinade, pepper, and salt.

4. For serving the steak, slice the steak. Arrange steak, sour cream, avocado, and cooked veggies in the tortillas. Serve with marinade and cilantro from the top.

Spaghetti Squash With Stuffed Lasagna

Total Prep & Cooking Time: Two hours

Yields: Four servings

Nutrition Facts: Calories: 280 | Protein: 23.1g | Carbs: 6.7g | Fat: 21.3g | Fiber: 0.2g

Ingredients

- One pound of Italian sausage
- One spaghetti squash
- One cup of pasta sauce (low-carb)
- One-fourth cup of ricotta
- One-third cup of mozzarella
- Half cup of parmesan
- Pepper and salt (according to taste)
- Parsley (for garnishing)

Method:

1. Cut spaghetti squash in half. Remove the seeds. Bake the squash in the oven with the cut side down in one inch of water. Bake for fifty minutes at 200 degrees Celsius.

2. Take a skillet and add the sausage. Cook until browned and add pasta sauce. Simmer for ten minutes and add seasonings.

3. Take out the baked squash and scrape the inside portion with the help of a fork. Add the squash strands in a bowl.

4. Combine the strands with ricotta, meat sauce, and cheese.

5. Stuff the squash shells with the mixture and arrange in a baking sheet. Top with mozzarella.

6. Bake the squash for fifteen minutes until the cheese melts.

7. Serve with parsley from the top.

Zucchini Boats With Stuffed Tuna

Total Prep & Cooking Time: Thirty minutes

Yields: Two servings

Nutrition Facts: Calories: 412 | Protein: 37.2g | Carbs: 23.2g | Fat: 18.3g | Fiber: 10.6g

Ingredients

- Two tsps. of avocado oil
- Half red bell pepper (diced)
- Two cans of wild tuna
- Half cup of salsa
- Two zucchinis
- Pepper and salt
- Half tsp. of cumin

For salsa:

- One avocado (cubed)
- One-fourth cup of cilantro (chopped)
- Three tbsps. of onion (minced)
- Two tsps. of lime juice

Method:

1. Take a frying pan and heat oil in it. Add diced pepper and sauté for two minutes. Remove the pepper and add tuna. Cook for four minutes.
2. Add salsa to the pan. Combine well.
3. Trim the zucchini ends. Slice them in half, lengthwise. Use a spoon for scraping out the flesh. Sprinkle some cumin, pepper, and salt.
4. Fill the zucchini shells with tuna mixture.
5. Preheat your oven at 200 degrees Celsius.
6. Bake the zucchini for twenty minutes.
7. Mix the ingredients for the salsa in a large small mixing bowl.
8. Serve the zucchini boats with salsa by the side.

Spinach and Goat Cheese Stuffed Breast of Chicken

Total Prep & Cooking Time: Forty-five minutes

Yields: Four servings

Nutrition Facts: Calories: 229 | Protein: 27.8g | Carbs: 4.9g | Fat: 13.7g | Fiber: 2.8g

Ingredients

- Four breasts of chicken
- Two tbsps. of olive oil
- Four cups of spinach
- Half tsp. of garlic powder
- Two ounces of goat cheese
- One onion (sliced)
- Eight ounces of bella mushrooms
- One tsp. of thyme
- Pepper and salt (for seasoning)

Method:

1. Heat the oven at 175 degrees Celsius.

2. Use a sharp knife for cutting slits on the upper side of the chicken breasts. Drizzle the breasts with olive oil, pepper, and salt. Keep aside.

3. Take a large skillet and heat half tbsp. of oil in it. Add spinach and cook for two minutes. Add garlic powder and cook until the spinach wilts.

4. Transfer spinach to a bowl. Add the goat cheese. Combine well.

5. Stuff the slits of the chicken breasts with the cheese and spinach mixture.

6. Heat one tbsp. of oil in the same skillet. Add mushrooms, onion, and thyme. Season with pepper and salt. Cook until the onions caramelize. Move the cooked veggies to a side to make some room for the chicken breasts.

7. Add the stuffed chicken breasts to the skillet.

8. Put the skillet in the oven. Bake for thirty minutes.

9. Serve hot.

Chapter 2: Quick and Easy Recipes

When you are short of time, opting for quick and easy recipes is the best option. So, I have included some easy recipes in this section that you can make without any hassle.

Antipasto Salad

Total Prep & Cooking Time: Thirty minutes

Yields: Two servings

Nutrition Facts: Calories: 510 | Protein: 36.8g | Carbs: 12.4g | Fat: 61g | Fiber: 10.6g

Ingredients

- Ten ounces of lettuce (chopped in pieces)
- Two tbsps. of parsley (chopped)
- Five ounces of mozzarella cheese (sliced)
- Three ounces of each
    - Salami (sliced thinly)
    - Prosciutto (sliced thinly)
- Four ounces of canned artichokes (quartered)
- Two cups of roasted red pepper
- One ounce of each
    - Sun-dried tomatoes (chopped)
    - Olives (sliced)
- One-third cup of basil

- One chili pepper (chopped)
- Half tbsp. of salt
- Four tbsps. of olive oil

Method:

1. Distribute the leaves of lettuce on serving plates or on a large dish.
2. Add parsley from the top.
3. Layer all the ingredients of antipasto.
4. In a bowl, mix chopped chili, basil, and salt. Crush the ingredients using a wooden spoon.
5. Sprinkle the crushed mixture over the salad and serve with olive oil from the top.

Feta Cheese and Chicken Plate

Total Prep & Cooking Time: Ten minutes

Yields: Two servings

Nutrition Facts: Calories: 810 | Protein: 63.3g | Carbs: 8.7g | Fat: 71g | Fiber: 3.2g

Ingredients

- Five-hundred grams of rotisserie chicken
- Two cups of feta cheese
- Two tomatoes
- Three cups of lettuce
- Ten olives
- One-third cup of olive oil
- Pepper and salt (according to taste)

Method:

1. Arrange chicken, lettuce, cheese, and olives on a plate. Slice the tomatoes and arrange them on the plate.
2. Sprinkle pepper and salt for seasoning.
3. Serve with olive oil from the top.

Note: If you do not want to use rotisserie chicken, you can cook the chicken from scratch.

Cheese Omelet

Total Prep & Cooking Time: Fifteen minutes

Yields: Two servings

Nutrition Facts: Calories: 797 | Protein: 37.2g | Carbs: 3.9g | Fat: 74.2g | Fiber: 0.1g

Ingredients

- Half cup of butter
- Six large eggs
- One cup of cheddar cheese (shredded)
- Pepper and salt (according to taste)

Method:

1. Break the eggs in a bowl. Add the cheese and whisk. Season with pepper and salt.
2. Take a medium-sized pan and melt some butter in it. Add the whisked egg mixture and allow it to set for two minutes.
3. Reduce the flame and cook for four minutes on each side. Add the leftover cheese.
4. Fold the omelet in half. Cook for one more minute.
5. Serve hot.

Baked Salmon and Pesto

Total Prep & Cooking Time: Thirty minutes

Yields: Four servings

Nutrition Facts: Calories: 625 | Protein: 48.3g | Carbs: 3.2g | Fat: 89g | Fiber: 0.7g

Ingredients

- Four tbsps. of pesto
- One cup of mayonnaise
- Half cup of Greek yogurt
- Pepper and salt (according to taste)

For the salmon:

- Four fillets of salmon
- Four tbsps. of green pesto
- Pepper and salt (for seasoning)

Method:

1. Grease a baking dish with some oil. Place the fillets of salmon on the dish with the skin-side down. Spread green pesto on the fillets and season with pepper and salt.

2. Bake the salmon for thirty minutes at 200 degrees Celsius.

3. Stir the ingredients for the sauce in a bowl.

4. Serve the salmon with sauce from the top.

Pork Chops and Blue Cheese Sauce

Total Prep & Cooking Time: Twenty minutes

Yields: Four servings

Nutrition Facts: Calories: 669 | Protein: 53.2g | Carbs: 4.3g | Fat: 60.1g | Fiber: 1.6g

Ingredients

- Two cups of blue cheese
- One cup of whipping cream (heavy)
- Four pork chops
- Seven ounces of green beans
- Two tbsps. of butter
- Pepper and salt

Method:

1. Crumble the blue cheese in a pot. Place the pot over medium flame and allow the cheese to melt.

2. Add whipping cream in the melted cheese and mix well. Simmer for two minutes.

3. Season the chops using pepper and salt.

4. Take an iron skillet and heat some oil in it. Add the chops and cook for four minutes on each side.

5. Add the juices from the pan in the sauce and stir.

6. Trim the beans. Heat some oil butter in the skillet and sauté the beans for two minutes.

7. Serve the pork chops with cheese sauce from the top and beans by the side.

Green Pepper and Pork Stir-Fry

Total Prep & Cooking Time: Twenty-five minutes

Yields: Two servings

Nutrition Facts: Calories: 678 | Protein: 31.2g | Carbs: 5.3g | Fat: 71.3g | Fiber: 4.6g

Ingredients

- Four ounces of butter
- Four-hundred grams of pork shoulder (cut in strips)
- Two bell pepper (green, sliced)
- Two scallions (sliced)
- Half cup of almond
- One tsp. of chili paste
- Pepper and salt

Method:

1. Heat butter in a wok. Add the meat strips in the butter and cook for five minutes until browned.
2. Add the chili paste along with veggies. Cook for two minutes. Add pepper and salt.
3. Serve the stir-fry with almonds from the top.

Broccoli With Fried Chicken

Total Prep & Cooking Time: Thirty minutes

Yields: Two servings

Nutrition Facts: Calories: 633 | Protein: 30.1g | Carbs: 5.3g | Fat: 64.3g | Fiber: 3.6g

Ingredients

- Nine ounces of broccoli
- One cup of butter
- Ten ounces of chicken thighs (boneless)
- Pepper and salt
- Half cup of mayonnaise

Method:

1. Rinse the broccoli thoroughly under running water. Trim the florets along with the stem.
2. Heat some butter in a pan.
3. Season the chicken thighs. Add the chicken to the pan and cook them for five minutes on all sides.
4. Add some more butter in the pan and add the broccoli. Toss the broccoli and chicken and cook for two minutes.
5. Serve with mayonnaise from the top.

Fried Eggs With Pork and Kale

Total Prep & Cooking Time: Twenty-five minutes

Yields: Three servings

Nutrition Facts: Calories: 910 | Protein: 24g | Carbs: 7.6g | Fat: 89g | Fiber: 6.3g

Ingredients

- One cup of kale
- Three ounces of butter
- Six ounces of bacon or pork belly (smoked)
- One ounce of walnuts
- Four large eggs
- Pepper and salt

Method:

1. Chop the kale and wash them under cold water.
2. Melt some butter in a skillet and cook the kale for two minutes until the edges are slightly browned.
3. Remove kale from the skillet and keep aside. Add bacon or pork belly in the same skillet and sear until crispy.
4. Add the kale in the skillet along with walnuts. Toss the ingredients.
5. Heat butter in another pan and fry the eggs sunny side up. Add pepper and salt for seasoning.
6. Serve the eggs with kale mixture by the side.

Chapter 3: Sweet Recipes

Even when you are on a diet, you don't have to compromise on satisfying your sweet tooth. So, I have included some easy to make sweet keto recipes in this section.

Sugar Cinnamon Donuts

Total Prep & Cooking Time: Twenty-five minutes

Yields: Twelve servings

Nutrition Facts: Calories: 82 | Protein: 2.3g | Carbs: 1.9g | Fat: 7.8g | Fiber: 0.3g

Ingredients

- Two eggs
- One-fourth cup of almond milk
- One-fourth tsp. of apple cider vinegar

- One tsp. of vanilla extract
- Two tbsps. of butter
- One-third cup of sweetener
- One cup of fine almond flour
- Half tbsp. of coconut flour
- One tsp. of cinnamon (ground)
- One and a half tsp. of baking powder
- Half tsp. of baking soda
- Half cup of salt

For sugar cinnamon coating:

- One-fourth cup of granulated erythritol
- One tsp. of cinnamon (ground)
- Two tbsps. of butter

Method:

1. Whisk together almond milk, eggs, butter, vinegar, vanilla extract, and sweetener. Combine until smooth.

2. Combine coconut flour, almond flour, baking powder, cinnamon, salt, and baking soda in a bowl. Add all the dry ingredients slowly to the mixture of wet ingredients. Stir well until combined.

3. Transfer the donut batter into a donut pan.

4. Bake the donuts for fifteen minutes at 175 degrees Celsius.

5. Take out the donuts and keep aside for cooling.

6. Stir together cinnamon and sweetener in a bowl.

7. Melt the butter in a pan.

8. Take the donuts and dunk them in the butter. Roll the donuts in the cinnamon coating.

Mug Brownie

Total Prep & Cooking Time: Ten minutes

Yields: Two servings

Nutrition Facts: Calories: 194 | Protein: 7.9g | Carbs: 7.6g | Fat: 16.5g | Fiber: 6.7g

Ingredients

- Two tbsps. of almond flour
- One tbsp. of each
    - Granulated sweetener
    - Cocoa powder
    - Almond butter
    - Chocolate chips
- One-eighth tsp. of baking powder
- Three tbsps. of milk

Method:

1. Use a cooking spray for greasing cereal bowls or mugs.
2. Combine the listed dry ingredients. Mix properly.
3. Mix milk and almond butter in a separate bowl and mix well.
4. Combine the dry and wet ingredients. Mix well. Add the chocolate chips and fold well.
5. Pour the batter in the cereal bowls. Bake for six minutes.
6. Enjoy your brownie from the bowl.

Mini Cheesecake

Total Prep & Cooking Time: Three hours and twenty minutes

Yields: Six servings

Nutrition Facts: Calories: 230 | Protein: 4.7g | Carbs: 5.1g | Fat: 19.6g | Fiber: 1.8g

Ingredients

For the crust:

- Half cup of almond flour
- Two tbsps. of sweetener
- Half tsp. of cinnamon
- Two tbsps. of butter (melted)

For the filling:

- Six ounces of cream cheese (softened)
- Five tbsps. of sweetener
- One-fourth cup of sour cream
- Half tsp. of vanilla extract
- One egg
- Two tsps. of cinnamon (ground)

For the frosting:

- One tbsp. of butter (softened)
- Three tbsps. of confectioners sweetener
- One-fourth tsp. of vanilla extract
- Two tsps. of heavy cream

Method:

1. Heat the oven at 175 degrees Celsius. Line a small muffin pan with six silicone liners.

2. Whisk almond flour, cinnamon, and sweetener in a bowl. Add melted butter and mix well.

3. Divide the prepared crust among the muffin cups. Press the crust to the bottom. Bake in the oven for five minutes.

4. Beat three tbsps. of sweetener along with the cream cheese in a bowl. Add vanilla, egg, and sour cream. Beat well.

5. Reduce oven temperature to 160 degrees Celsius.

6. Whisk cinnamon and butter in a bowl.

7. Add three-fourth tbsp. of cheese mixture into the muffin cups. Sprinkle cinnamon mixture from the top.

8. Bake the muffins for fifteen minutes. Refrigerate the muffins for two hours.

9. Beat powdered sweetener and butter in a bowl. Add heavy cream and vanilla extract. Mix well.

10. Transfer the frosting to a zip-lock bag and cut a small hole at the corner.

11. Add frosting over the cheesecakes.

Keto Fudge

Total Prep & Cooking Time: One hour

Yields: Twelve servings

Nutrition Facts: Calories: 158 | Protein: 0.1g | Carbs: 0.6g | Fat: 17.9g | Fiber: 0.7g

Ingredients

- One cup of coconut oil
- One-fourth cup of each
    - Cocoa powder
    - Erythritol (powdered)
- One tsp. of vanilla extract
- One-eighth tsp. of sea salt
- Sea salt

Method:

1. Use parchment paper for lining a glass baking dish.
2. Beat sweetener and coconut oil using a hand blender. Make sure the mixture is fluffy.
3. Add vanilla extract, cocoa powder, and salt. Combine well.
4. Pour the fudge mixture in the lined dish. Smoothen the top using a spoon or spatula.
5. Refrigerate the fudge for forty minutes until it solidifies.
6. Use a sharp knife to run along the edges of the dish for taking out the fudge.
7. Cut in small cubes and serve.

Peanut Butter Hearts

Total Prep & Cooking Time: Thirty minutes

Yields: Twenty servings

Nutrition Facts: Calories: 91 | Protein: 5.1g | Carbs: 7.1g | Fat: 6.7g | Fiber: 3.2g

Ingredients

- Two cups of peanut butter
- Three-fourth cup of any sticky sweetener
- One cup of coconut flour
- One and a half cup of chocolate chips

Method:

1. Use parchment paper for lining a large glass tray.
2. Combine sticky sweetener with peanut butter on the stovetop. Combine the mixture until it melts completely.
3. Add the coconut flour and combine. In case the batter is very thin, you can add more flour.
4. Make twenty balls from the dough. Use a heart-shaped cookie cutter for pressing the dough balls for making heart shape.
5. Arrange the hearts on the lined glass tray and refrigerate.
6. Melt the chocolate chips and dip the hearts in the melted chocolate.
7. Refrigerate again for twenty minutes until firm.

Peanut Butter and White Chocolate Blondies

Total Prep & Cooking Time: Three hours and thirty-five minutes

Yields: Sixteen servings

Nutrition Facts: Calories: 102 | Protein: 3.2g | Carbs: 2.2g | Fat: 9.3g | Fiber: 1.9g

Ingredients

- Half cup of each
    - Peanut butter
    - Sweetener of your choice
- Four tbsps. of butter (softened)
- Two large eggs
- One tsp. of vanilla extract
- Three tbsps. of cocoa butter (melted)
- One-fourth cup of almond flour
- One tbsp. of coconut flour
- One cup of cocoa butter (chopped)

Method:

1. Heat the oven at 175 degrees Celsius. Use a cooking spray for greasing a baking dish.
2. Combine all the ingredients in a large bowl using a hand mixer.
3. Pour the mixture in the greased dish.
4. Bake for thirty minutes.
5. Cool the blondies and refrigerate for about three hours.
6. Cut the blondies in squares and serve.

Low Carb Ice Cream

Total Prep & Cooking Time: Five hours and thirty-five minutes

Yields: Eight servings

Nutrition Facts: Calories: 337 | Protein: 2.2g | Carbs: 3.1g | Fat: 34g | Fiber: 0.3g

Ingredients

- Three tbsps. of butter
- Three cups of heavy cream
- One-third cup of powdered allulose
- One-fourth cup of coconut oil
- One tsp. of vanilla extract
- One medium-sized bean of vanilla

Method:

1. Take a pan and heat it over medium flame. Melt butter in it. Add a two-third cup of the heavy cream along with sweetener. Boil the mixture and simmer for thirty minutes.

2. Pour the mixture in a bowl and let it cool at room temperature. Add vanilla seeds from the bean along with the vanilla extract. Add coconut oil and mix well.

3. Add the remaining cream and combine until smooth.

4. Pour the mixture in a container and use a spatula for smoothening the top.

5. Freeze the ice cream for five hours. Ensure that you stir the ice cream mixture after every thirty minutes for the first two hours and then after every sixty minutes.

Chocolate Donut

Total Prep & Cooking Time: One hour and twenty-five minutes

Yields: Ten servings

Nutrition Facts: Calories: 219 | Protein: 5.1g | Carbs: 7.6g | Fat: 18.6g | Fiber: 3.1g

Ingredients

- Four eggs
- Half cup of butter (melted)
- Three tbsps. of milk
- One tsp. of stevia
- One-fourth cup of each
    - Coconut flour
    - Cocoa powder (unsweetened)
    - Sea salt
    - Baking soda

For the glaze:

- One tbsp. of avocado oil
- Three-fourth cup of chocolate chips

Method:

1. Heat the oven at 175 degrees Celsius.
2. Use a cooking spray for greasing donut pan of ten cavities.
3. Mix melted butter, eggs, and stevia, and milk in a bowl.
4. Add cocoa powder, coconut flour, baking soda, and salt.
5. Pour the mixture in the donut pan. Bake the donuts for fifteen minutes until set.
6. Let the donuts cool for fifteen minutes.
7. Add the chocolate chips in a bowl and melt in the microwave. Add avocado oil and stir.
8. Take out the donuts and dip them in the chocolate glaze.
9. Let the donuts sit for thirty minutes.

Chapter 4: Savory Recipes

In this section, I have included some tasty savory keto recipes that you can enjoy at any time of the day. So, let's have a look at them.

Keto McMuffin

Total Prep & Cooking Time: Twenty minutes

Yields: Two servings

Nutrition Facts: Calories: 610 | Protein: 24g | Carbs: 3.2g | Fat: 51.8g | Fiber: 6.9g

Ingredients

- One-fourth cup of each
    - Almond flour
    - Flaxmeal
- One-fourth tsp. of baking soda
- One egg
- Two tbsps. of heavy whipping cream
- One cup of cheddar cheese (shredded)
- Three tbsps. of water
- Salt (for seasoning)

For the filling:

- Two large eggs
- One tbsp. of butter
- Two cheddar cheese slices
- One tsp. of Dijon mustard
- Pepper and salt (for seasoning)

Method:

1. Combine all the dry ingredients. Mix well.
2. Add cream, water, and egg. Combine well using a fork.
3. Add the shredded cheese and mix.
4. Pour the mixture in greased ramekins. Microwave the mixture at high settings for two minutes.
5. Take a pan and fry the eggs. Add pepper and salt for seasoning.
6. Cut the prepared muffins in half. Spread butter on the inside portion of the muffin halves.
7. Top the muffin slices with egg, cheese, and mustard.
8. Serve immediately.

Sausage Hash With Rainbow Chard

Total Prep & Cooking Time: Twenty-five minutes

Yields: Two servings

Nutrition Facts: Calories: 570 | Protein: 25g | Carbs: 7.6g | Fat: 44.6g | Fiber: 5.6g

Ingredients

- Two-hundred grams of Swiss chard
- Two cups of cauliflower rice
- One-hundred and fifty grams of sausage meat
- Three tbsps. of lard
- Two garlic cloves (chopped)
- One tbsp. of lemon juice
- One tsp. of Dijon mustard
- Pepper and salt
- Four poached eggs

Method:

1. Chop the chard stalks into small pieces.

2. Take a greased skillet and add the sausage meat. Cook for five minutes until browned. Keep aside

3. Add the remaining lard to the same skillet. Add the garlic. Cook for one minute and add the cauliflower rice. Cook the mixture for five minutes.

4. Add the chard and Dijon mustard. Combine well. Add lemon juice and cook the mixture for two minutes. Add pepper and salt for seasoning.

5. Add the sausage meat and mix.

6. Serve with poached eggs.

Veggie and Chicken Sausage Skillet

Total Prep & Cooking Time: Thirty minutes

Yields: Four servings

Nutrition Facts: Calories: 310 | Protein: 21g | Carbs: 9.3g | Fat: 22.3g | Fiber: 2.4g

Ingredients

- Three tbsps. of butter
- Five links of chicken sausage (sliced)
- Two garlic cloves (minced)
- One red onion (cut in chunks)
- One zucchini (sliced in rounds)
- One summer squash (sliced in rounds)
- One red capsicum (cut in chunks)
- One yellow capsicum (cut in chunks)
- Six cremini mushrooms (quartered)
- Half tsp. of each
    - Red pepper flakes (crushed)
    - Italian seasoning
- Pepper and salt

Method:

1. Take an iron skillet and melt some butter in it.

2. Add the sausage, onion, and garlic. Sauté the mixture for ten minutes.

3. Add the veggies and mix well. Add pepper flakes, Italian seasoning, pepper, and salt.

4. Sauté the mixture for fifteen minutes and serve hot.

Cheese and Crispy Salami

Total Prep & Cooking Time: Twenty-five minutes

Yields: Ten servings

Nutrition Facts: Calories: 37 | Protein: 2.3g | Carbs: 1.3g | Fat: 2.7g | Fiber: 6.3g

Ingredients

- Two ounces of dried salami
- One ounce of cream cheese
- Half cup of parsley (chopped)

Method:

1. Heat the oven at 170 degrees Celsius.
2. Slice the salami into thirty slices of a quarter inch.
3. Arrange the salami on a baking pan.
4. Bake them for fifteen minutes.
5. Top the salami with cream cheese along with parsley.

Buffalo Chicken Sandwich

Total Prep & Cooking Time: Twenty-five minutes

Yields: Four servings

Nutrition Facts: Calories: 480 | Protein: 27g | Carbs: 5.1g | Fat: 30g | Fiber: 2.2g

Ingredients

- Two cups of cooked chicken (shredded)
- One-third cup of red pepper sauce
- Three tbsps. of butter
- One-fourth tsp. of each
    - Celery seed spice
    - Sea salt
    - Garlic powder
- Two tbsps. of each
    - Blue cheese crumbles
    - Celery (minced)
- Four tbsps. of ranch dressing
- Three tbsps. of mayonnaise
- Four sandwich buns

Method:

1. Take a medium saucepan and melt butter in it. Add celery seed spice, red pepper sauce, sea salt, and garlic powder. Stir well.

2. Add the chicken along with celery to the pan. Mix well and cook for two minutes.

3. Add the mayonnaise and combine.

4. Cut the buns in half. Add half cup of prepared chicken mixture on the buns. Top the chicken with one tbsp. of ranch dressing and half tbsp. of cheese crumbles.

5. Place the other halves on top and serve.

Cream Cheese and Salmon Bites
Total Prep & Cooking Time: Twenty minutes

Yields: Ten servings

Nutrition Facts: Calories: 43 | Protein: 1.3g | Carbs: 0.3g | Fat: 4.6g | Fiber: 0.6g

Ingredients

- Two eggs
- Half cup of cream
- One tbsp. of salt
- One cup of cheese (shredded)
- One-third tsp. of dill (dried)
- One-third cup of cream cheese (diced)
- Two cups of salmon (smoked, chopped)

Method:

1. Combine cream, eggs, and salt in a bowl.

2. Add cheese, cream cheese, and dill. Mix well.

3. Grease a muffin tray with butter.

4. Pour the mixture in the muffin tray. Add some pieces of salmon into each muffin.

5. Bake the mixture in the oven for twenty minutes at 180 degrees Celsius.

6. Remove the bites and serve warm. Vegetable Turkey Pesto Bolognese

Total Prep & Cooking Time: Thirty minutes

Yields: Four servings

Nutrition Facts: Calories: 270 | Protein: 20.1g | Carbs: 4.3g | Fat: 13.2g | Fiber: 1.6g

Ingredients

- Two tsps. of oil
- One pound of turkey (ground)
- One cup of onion (diced)
- Two cups of each
    - Mushrooms (sliced)
    - Zucchini (sliced)
- Three tbsps. of pesto sauce
- Pasta of your choice (cooked)
- Grated cheese

Method:

1. Take a large skillet and add some oil. Add the turkey and cook until browned. Keep aside.
2. Add onions in the same and cook for two minutes. Add mushrooms and zucchini. Mix well.
3. Add the cooked turkey and combine it. Add pesto sauce simmer for five minutes.
4. Add cooked pasta along with cheese. Stir to combine. Simmer for two minutes.
5. Serve hot.

Turkey Patties

Total Prep & Cooking Time: Thirty minutes

Yields: Four servings

Nutrition Facts: Calories: 435 | Protein: 24g | Carbs: 4.5g | Fat: 37.2g | Fiber: 2.5g

Ingredients

- Five-hundred grams of ground turkey
- Half cup of almond flour
- One hot chili pepper (finely chopped)
- Two tsps. of Dijon mustard
- Two tbsps. of each
    - Parsley (chopped)
    - Lemon juice
    - Basil (chopped)
- Half tsp. of sea salt
- One tsp. black pepper (ground)
- Two spring onions (sliced finely)
- Two tbsps. of lard
- One egg
- Two garlic cloves (crushed)

Method:

1. Combine turkey, eggs, almond flour, garlic, pepper, lemon juice, Dijon mustard, basil, parsley, black pepper, and salt. Add the spring onions and mix well.

2. Make small patties using your hands.

3. Heat lard in a pan and add the patties. Cook the patties for five minutes on each side.

4. Let the patties sit for two minutes. Serve warm with spring onions.

Chapter 5: Poultry and Meat Recipes

Meat and poultry are rich in protein and various other nutrients that you need for perfect health. In this section, you will find some tasty poultry and meat keto recipes that you can make at home.

Beef Cabbage Skillet

Total Prep & Cooking Time: Thirty minutes

Yields: Four servings

Nutrition Facts: Calories: 357 | Protein: 13g | Carbs: 27g | Fat: 7.2g | Fiber: 11.3g

Ingredients

- Half green cabbage (shredded)
- Two tbsps. of butter
- One pound of beef (ground)
- Three tbsps. of taco seasoning
- One tsp. of minced onion (dried)
- One and a half cup of Mexican cheese blend
- Pepper and salt (according to taste)

Method:

1. Take a large skillet and heat one tbsp. of butter in it. Add shredded cabbage and sauté for two minutes. Keep aside.

2. Add one tbsp. of butter in the same skillet. Add the beef. Add onion, taco seasoning, and mix well. Cook for five minutes. Add one-fourth cup of water. Add the cooked cabbage along with pepper and salt. Combine half a cup of cheese.

3. Top with leftover cheese and place the skillet in the oven. Bake for ten minutes or until the cheese melts.

Meatball Casserole

Total Prep & Cooking Time: Three hours and thirty minutes

Yields: Six servings

Nutrition Facts: Calories: 470 | Protein: 37g | Carbs: 5.4g | Fat: 33.2g | Fiber: 4.7g

Ingredients

- Two pounds of beef (ground)
- Half cup of each
    - Mozzarella cheese
    - Parmesan cheese
- Two tbsps. of coconut flour
- Two large eggs
- Three-fourth tsp. of each
    - Onion (minced)
    - Salt
- One-fourth tsp. of Italian seasoning
- Half tsp. of garlic powder
- Twenty ounce can of spaghetti sauce
- Two cups of mozzarella cheese
- One tsp. of dried basil

Method:

1. Mix the ingredients in a bowl except for the spaghetti sauce, basil, and two cups of mozzarella cheese.
2. Heat a skillet on medium flame. Add one-fourth inch of coconut oil in the skillet.
3. Scoop meatballs from the mixture and add them to the skillet.
4. Cook the meatballs for five minutes until browned.
5. Place the meatballs in the base of a crockpot.
6. Add spaghetti sauce from the top.
7. Cook the meatballs on high for three hours.
8. Take out the meatballs in a baking dish.
9. Sprinkle cheese from the top.
10. Broil the meatballs for three minutes until cheese melts.

Beef Taquitos

Total Prep & Cooking Time: Forty minutes

Yields: Six servings

Nutrition Facts: Calories: 229 | Protein: 15.7g | Carbs: 1.6g | Fat: 16.3g | Fiber: 0.3g

Ingredients

- One cup of each
    - Cheddar cheese (shredded)
    - Mozzarella cheese (shredded)
- Half cup of parmesan cheese (grated)
- Half pound of beef (ground)
- One-fourth cup of onion (minced)
- Half tsp. of each
    - Paprika
    - Chili powder
    - Salt
    - Onion powder
    - Garlic powder
- One tsp. of cumin
- One-fourth tsp. of pepper
- One-third cup of water

Method:

1. Mix chili powder, cumin, garlic powder, onion powder, pepper, salt in a cup, and some water.
2. Take a skillet and brown the beef along with the onion. Add the mixture over the beef and simmer for ten minutes.
3. Mix all the cheese in a bowl. Divide the mixture of cheese for making six balls. Use parchment paper to line a baking sheet. Place them on the sheet and bake for eight minutes.
4. Let the cheese sheets cool down for two minutes.
5. Take one spoon of the beef mixture and place it on the edge of the cheese sheets. Repeat for the remaining sheets.
6. Roll them tightly for making cigar shape.
7. Serve warm.

Chicken Wings

Total Prep & Cooking Time: Fifty minutes

Yields: Four servings

Nutrition Facts: Calories: 287 | Protein: 2.3g | Carbs: 12g | Fat: 16.3g | Fiber: 1.9g

Ingredients

- Two pounds of chicken wings
- Two tsps. of salt
- Three-fourth cup of coconut aminos
- One-fourth tsp. of each

- Onion powder
- Ginger (ground)
- Garlic powder
- Chili flakes

Method:

1. Place the wings on a baking tray.

2. Sprinkle some salt evenly on the wings.

3. Bake the chicken wings in the oven for forty minutes at 180 degrees Celsius.

4. Take a skillet and add coconut aminos. Add garlic powder, ginger, onion powder, and chili flakes. Simmer the sauce and stir until the sauce thickens.

5. Place the cooked wings in a large bowl and pour the sauce over the wings. Toss the cooked wings in the prepared sauce. Coat evenly.

6. Serve hot.

Roasted Leg of Chicken

Total Prep & Cooking Time: One hour and ten minutes

Yields: Four servings

Nutrition Facts: Calories: 687 | Protein: 27.9g | Carbs: 10.1g | Fat: 58.9g | Fiber: 6g

Ingredients

- Four legs of chicken
- Four tbsps. of olive oil
- Two tbsps. of Italian seasoning
- Pepper and salt
- Twenty ounces of each
    - Cherry tomatoes
    - Broccoli

For the garlic butter:

- Four ounces of butter
- Two cloves of garlic (smashed)
- Pepper and salt

Method:

1. Toss the legs of the chicken with seasoning and oil.

2. Place the chicken legs in a baking sheet along with the tomatoes. Bake for forty-five minutes at 150 degrees Celsius.

3. As the chicken is cooking, cut the broccoli. Divide the florets and also slice the stem. Boil them in water for five minutes, along with some salt. Drain the broccoli water.

4. For making the garlic butter, combine all the ingredients in a small bowl.

5. Serve the cooked chicken legs with tomatoes, broccoli, and garlic butter by the side.

Note: Place the chicken legs in the oven with the skin side up.

Chapter 6: Staple Recipes

In this section, I have included some simple keto recipes made from everyday staples. Let's have a look at them.

Keto Waffles

Total Prep & Cooking Time: Ten minutes

Yields: Two servings

Nutrition Facts: Calories: 160 | Protein: 21.3g | Carbs: 12.6g | Fat: 5.6g | Fiber: 10.3g

Ingredients

- Four tbsps. of coconut flour
- One tbsp. of each
    - Granulated sweetener
    - Apple sauce (unsweetened)
- One-fourth tsp. of each
    - Baking powder
    - Cinnamon
- Two-third cup of egg whites
- One-fourth cup of milk
- Half tsp. of vanilla extract
- One tsp. of coconut oil

Method:

1. Take a mixing bowl and mix the dry ingredients. Keep aside.

2. Add egg whites, vanilla extract, milk, and apple sauce in a bowl. Pour this mixture into the mixture of dry ingredients. Mix well.

3. Heat a waffle iron and grease with cooking spray or oil.

4. Add the waffle batter and cook for five minutes until fluffy and crisp.

Cookie Dough

Total Prep & Cooking Time: Ten minutes

Yields: Four servings

Nutrition Facts: Calories: 130 | Protein: 4.6g | Carbs: 4.3g | Fat: 12g | Fiber: 2.9g

Ingredients

- Half cup of almond flour
- Two tbsps. of each
    - Sticky sweetener
    - Granulated sweetener
    - Coconut flour
- One and a half tbsp. of coconut oil
- One tbsp. of chocolate chips

Method:

1. Combine coconut flour, almond flour, and granulated sugar in a bowl.
2. Add coconut oil and sticky sweetener. Mix well. Add the chocolate chips.
3. You can either enjoy the dough immediately or refrigerate it for thirty minutes.

Baked Tofu

Total Prep & Cooking Time: One hour and ten minutes

Yields: Two servings

Nutrition Facts: Calories: 131.3 | Protein: 11.3g | Carbs: 3.1g | Fat: 8.6g | Fiber: 1.7g

Ingredients

- One block of tofu (firm)
- One tbsp. of each
    - Soy sauce
    - Sesame oil
    - Tamari
- Half tsp. of each
    - Ginger
    - Garlic powder
    - Cayenne powder

Method:

1. Mix all the listed ingredients except for the tofu. Let the marinade sit for five minutes.

2. Chop the block of tofu into small pieces. Add the tofu cubes in the marinade. Refrigerate for half an hour.

3. Use parchment paper for lining a baking tray. Add the marinated tofu and bake for thirty minutes. Flip the tofu cubes halfway.

4. Serve immediately.

Cauliflower Fried Rice

Total Prep & Cooking Time: Twenty minutes

Yields: Four servings

Nutrition Facts: Calories: 135 | Protein: 7.9g | Carbs: 10.3g | Fat: 7.6g | Fiber: 8.6g

Ingredients

- Two tbsps. of sesame oil
- Two garlic cloves (finely chopped)
- One onion (finely chopped)
- Two scallions
- One-fourth cup of carrots (finely chopped)
- Eight cups of cauliflower rice
- Half cup of soy sauce
- One-fourth tsp. of cayenne pepper

Method:

1. Take a large wok and heat it over a medium flame. Add some oil in it. Add garlic and onion. Cook for two minutes. Add scallions and carrots. Sauté for two minutes.

2. Add the cauliflower rice and combine well. Add cayenne and soy sauce. Fry for four minutes.

3. Serve the fried rice with scallions from the top.

PART II

Air Fryer Recipes

The air fryer is a new mode of cooking advertised as a guilt-free and healthy way of enjoying all your favorite foods. Air fryer cooking claims that it can lower the fat content of various well-known food items such as chicken wings, French fries, fish sticks, and others. But, how healthy is it to cook in an air fryer?

Air fryer is a trendy appliance in the kitchen today that is being used for making food items like pastries, meat, and potato chips. It functions by simply circulating the hot air all around the food for producing crispy and crunchy exterior. All those food items that are air-fried are believed to be great alternatives for the deep-fried food items. There is no need to submerge the food items in oil. Just brush some oil, and you are good to go. It has been found that air fryer can cut off the fat content by 75%. The main reason behind this is that they need less amount of fat in comparison to deep fryers. For example, most of the deep-fried food items will require three cups of oil. But, the same can be cooked in an air fryer with only one tbsp. of oil.

In case you are willing to trim some extra fat around your waistline, substituting deep-fried food items with air-fried food items is a great way to start. So, it can be said that air-fryer can help in promoting weight loss. Frying food can produce dangerous compounds such as acrylamide. Cooking food in an air fryer can help you cut down the acrylamide content in your cooking.

I have included some tasty air fryer recipes in this chapter that can be made with minimal effort.

Chapter 1: Chicken And Pork Recipes

Meat forms an essential part of most types of diet. Here are some chicken and pork recipes that can be made easily using an air fryer.

Maple Chicken Thighs
Total Prep & Cooking Time: One hour and thirty-five minutes

Yields: Four servings

Nutrition Facts: Calories: 410 | Protein: 22.3g | Carbs: 47.9g | Fat: 12.3g | Fiber: 1.2g

Ingredients

- One cup of buttermilk
- One large egg
- Half cup of maple syrup
- One tsp. of garlic (granulated)
- Four chicken thighs

For the dry mix:

- Half cup of flour
- One-fourth cup of tapioca flour
- One tbsp. of salt

- One tsp. of each
    - Sweet paprika
    - Onion (granulated)
    - Honey powder
- Half tsp. of paprika (smoked)
- One-fourth tsp. of each
    - Garlic (granulated)
    - Cayenne powder
    - Black pepper (ground)

Method:

1. Mix maple syrup, buttermilk, egg, and one tsp. of granulated garlic in a bowl. Add the thighs of chicken and marinate them for one hour.

2. Mix tapioca flour, flour, sweet paprika, salt, smoked paprika, pepper, granulated onion, half tsp. of granulated garlic, cayenne, and honey powder in a bowl.

3. Preheat your air fryer at 190 degrees Celsius.

4. Drain the marinade. Add the thighs in the flour mixture. Place chicken thighs in the air fryer basket. Cook them for ten minutes. Flip the chicken thighs and cook again for ten minutes.

Buttermilk Chicken

Total Prep & Cooking Time: Thirty-five minutes

Yields: Four servings

Nutrition Facts: Calories: 331 | Protein: 23.2g | Carbs: 26.3g | Fat: 10.6g | Fiber: 0.8g

Ingredients

- One cup of buttermilk
- Half tsp. of each
    - Hot sauce
    - Garlic salt
    - Paprika
    - Oregano
    - Onion powder
- One-third cup of tapioca flour
- One-eighth tsp. of black pepper (ground)
- One large egg
- Half cup of flour
- Two tsps. of brown sugar
- One tsp. of garlic powder
- One-fourth tsp. of black pepper
- One pound of chicken thighs (skinless, boneless)

Method:

1. Take a shallow dish and mix hot sauce with buttermilk.

2. Combine garlic salt, tapioca flour, and one-eighth tsp. of black pepper. Mix well.

3. Beat the egg in a bowl.

4. Mix salt, flour, brown sugar, paprika, garlic powder, onion powder, one-fourth tsp. of black pepper, and oregano in a bowl. Combine well.

5. Dip the thighs of chicken in this order: mixture of buttermilk, mixture of tapioca flour, beaten egg, and flour mixture.

6. Preheat your air fryer at 190 degrees Celsius. Use parchment paper for lining the fryer basket.

7. Cook the chicken thighs for ten minutes. Flip the thighs and cook again for ten minutes.

Cheddar-Stuffed BBQ Breasts of Chicken

Total Prep & Cooking Time: Thirty-five minutes

Yields: Two servings

Nutrition Facts: Calories: 370 | Protein: 35.7g | Carbs: 11.7g | Fat: 17.7g | Fiber: 0.6g

Ingredients

- Three bacon strips
- Two ounces of cheddar cheese (cubed)
- One-fourth cup of barbeque sauce
- Two chicken breasts (skinless)
- Pepper and salt

Method:

1. Preheat your air fryer to 190 degrees Celsius. Cook a bacon strip in the air fryer for two minutes. Chop one strip of bacon. Use parchment paper for lining the fryer basket.

2. Mix cooked bacon, one tbsp. of barbeque sauce, and cheddar cheese.

3. Create a one-inch pouch at the top of the chicken breasts. Stuff the pouch with the mixture of bacon and cheese.

4. Wrap the bacon strips around the breasts of chicken. Use barbeque sauce for coating the chicken breasts.

5. Cook for ten minutes in the air fryer. Flip the chicken breasts and cook again for ten minutes.

Buffalo Chicken

Total Prep & Cooking Time: Forty minutes

Yields: Four servings

Nutrition Facts: Calories: 230 | Protein: 30.2g | Carbs: 21.1g | Fat: 4.7g | Fiber: 1.9g

Ingredients

- Half cup of Greek yogurt
- One-fourth cup of egg substitute
- One tbsp. of each
    - Hot sauce
    - Sweet paprika
    - Cayenne pepper
    - Garlic pepper seasoning
- One tsp. of hot sauce
- One cup of bread crumbs
- One pound of chicken breast

Method:

1. Mix egg substitute, yogurt, and hot sauce in a mixing bowl.
2. Combine paprika, bread crumbs, cayenne pepper, and garlic pepper in a dish.
3. Dip the chicken breasts into the mixture of yogurt and coat in the mixture of bread crumbs.
4. Cook the chicken breasts in the air fryer for eight minutes. Flip the chicken breasts and cook again for five minutes.

Breaded Pork Chops

Total Prep & Cooking Time: Twenty minutes

Yields: Four servings

Nutrition Facts: Calories: 390 | Protein: 41.7g | Carbs: 10.3g | Fat: 17.1g | Fiber: 0.9g

Ingredients

- Four pork chops
- One tsp. of Cajun seasoning
- Two cups of garlic and cheese flavored croutons
- Two large eggs
- One cooking spray

Method:

1. Place the chops in a dish and season with the Cajun seasoning.
2. Add the croutons in a blender and pulse them.
3. Beat the eggs in a shallow dish.
4. Dip the pork chops into the beaten eggs and then coat in the blended croutons.
5. Use a cooking spray for misting the pork chops.
6. Cook the chops for five minutes. Flip the chops and cook again for five minutes.

Pork Meatballs

Total Prep & Cooking Time: Thirty-five minutes

Yields: Twelve servings

Nutrition Facts: Calories: 120 | Protein: 8.4g | Carbs: 3.9g | Fat: 7.7g | Fiber: 0.3g

Ingredients

- Twelve ounces of pork (ground)
- Eight ounces of Italian sausage (ground)
- Half cup of panko bread crumbs
- One large egg
- One tsp. of each
  - Parsley (dried)
  - Salt
- Half tsp. of paprika

Method:

1. Combine sausage, pork, egg, bread crumbs, salt, paprika, and parsley in a bowl. Mix well. Make twelve meatballs using your hands.
2. Place the meatballs in the basket of the air fryer basket. Cook them for eight minutes. Shake the fryer basket and cook again for two minutes.

Pork Jerky

Total Prep & Cooking Time: Eleven hours and ten minutes

Yields: Forty servings

Nutrition Facts: Calories: 56 | Protein: 4.4g | Carbs: 0.2g | Fat: 4.6g | Fiber: 0.1g

Ingredients

- Two pounds of pork (ground)
- One tbsp. of each
    - Sesame oil
    - Sriracha
    - Soy sauce
    - Rice vinegar
- Half tsp. of each
    - Salt
    - Black pepper
    - Onion powder
    - Pink curing salt

Method:

1. Mix pork, sriracha, sesame oil, soy sauce, vinegar, pepper, salt, onion powder, and curing salt in a bowl. Mix well and refrigerate for eight hours.
2. Use a jerky gun for making as many jerky sticks as possible.
3. Cook the jerky sticks in the fryer rack for one hour.
4. Flip the sticks and cook again for one hour.
5. Repeat step number four for three hours.
6. Transfer the sticks to a paper towel and soak excess fat.
7. Serve immediately, or you can store the sticks in the refrigerator for one month.

Pork Skewers

Total Prep & Cooking Time: Forty minutes

Yields: Forty servings

Nutrition Facts: Calories: 310 | Protein: 21g | Carbs: 30.6g | Fat: 9.2g | Fiber: 8.9g

Ingredients

- Two tbsps. of white sugar
- Five tsps. of onion powder
- Four tsps. of thyme (dried, crushed)
- One tbsp. of each
  - Black pepper (ground)
  - Allspice (ground)
  - Vegetable oil
  - Honey
  - Cilantro (chopped)
- Two tsps. of each
  - Salt
  - Cayenne pepper
- Three-fourth tsp. of nutmeg (ground)
- One-fourth tsp. of cloves (ground)
- One-fourth cup of coconut (shredded)
- One pound of pork tenderloin (cut in cubes of one inch)
- Four skewers
- One mango (peeled, chopped)
- Half a can of black beans (rinsed)
- One cup of red onion (chopped)
- Three tbsps. of lime juice
- One-eighth tsp. of black pepper (ground)

Method:

1. Mix onion powder, sugar, allspice, thyme, black pepper, salt, cayenne pepper, cloves, and nutmeg in a bowl. Transfer the prepared rub to another bowl and reserve one tbsp. for the pork. Add shredded coconut to the one tbsp. of rub and mix.

2. Preheat your air fryer to 175 degrees Celsius.

3. Start threading the chunks of pork onto the skewers. Use some oil for brushing the pork and then sprinkle the rub on all sides. Place the prepared skewers in the air fryer basket.

4. Cook for eight minutes.

5. Mash one-third of the mango in a bowl and add black beans, lime juice, onion, remaining mango, cilantro, honey, pepper, and salt.

6. Serve the pork skewers with mango mixture by the side.

Pork Tenderloin With Mustard Crust

Total Prep & Cooking Time: Forty minutes

Yields: Forty servings

Nutrition Facts: Calories: 280 | Protein: 24.3g | Carbs: 30.2g | Fat: 6.1g | Fiber: 4.9g

Ingredients

- One-fourth cup of Dijon mustard
- Two tbsps. of brown sugar
- One tsp. of parsley flakes
- Half tsp. of thyme (dried)
- One-fourth tsp. of each
    - Black pepper (ground)
    - Salt
- Two pounds of pork tenderloin
- One pound of small potatoes
- Twelve ounces of green beans (trimmed)
- One tbsp. of olive oil

Method:

1. Start by preheating your air fryer at 200 degrees Celsius.
2. Combine brown sugar, mustard, thyme, parsley, pepper, and salt together in a bowl. Coat the tenderloins with the marinade evenly on all sides.
3. Combine green beans, potatoes, and olive oil in another bowl. Use pepper and salt for seasoning.
4. Cook the pork for twenty minutes. Flip the pork and cook again for five minutes.
5. Let the pork sit for ten minutes.
6. Cook potatoes and green beans for ten minutes in the air fryer.
7. Serve pork with green beans and potatoes by the side.

Chapter 2: Beef And Fish Recipes

There are various types of beef and fish recipes that can be made using an air fryer. Let's have a look at them.

Beef Tenderloin

Total Prep & Cooking Time: One hour

Yields: Eight servings

Nutrition Facts: Calories: 230.2 | Protein: 31.2g | Carbs: 0.2g | Fat: 10.3g | Fiber: 0.1g

Ingredients

- Two pounds of beef tenderloin
- One tbsp. of each
    - Oregano (dried)
    - Vegetable oil
- One tsp. of salt
- Half tsp. of black pepper (cracked)

Method:

1. Preheat your air fryer at 200 degrees Celsius.
2. Use a paper towel to dry the beef tenderloin.
3. Drizzle some oil over the tenderloin and sprinkle pepper, oregano, and salt. Rub all the spices along with the oil evenly on the meat.
4. Reduce the air fryer heat to 190 degrees Celsius and cook the beef for twenty minutes. Reduce the air fryer heat to 180 degrees Celsius. Cook again for ten minutes.
5. Let the beef rest for ten minutes.
6. Slice the tenderloin and serve warm.

Beef Wontons

Total Prep & Cooking Time: Thirty minutes

Yields: Twenty-four servings

Nutrition Facts: Calories: 73.2 | Protein: 4.4g | Carbs: 5.9g | Fat: 2.6g | Fiber: 0.3g

Ingredients

- One pound of lean beef (ground)
- Two tbsps. of green onion (chopped)
- Half tsp. of each
    - Garlic powder
    - Salt
- One-fourth tsp. of each
    - Ginger (ground)
    - Black pepper (ground)
- Sixteen ounces of wonton wrappers
- Two tbsps. of sesame oil

Method:

1. Mix green onions, beef, garlic powder, salt, ginger, and pepper in a large bowl.

2. Preheat your air fryer at 175 degrees Celsius.

3. Place the wrappers on a large plate.

4. Take one tbsp. of the prepared beef mixture and add it to the wonton wrapper. Wet your finger with some water and fold the wrappers in half for forming a triangle.

5. Use sesame oil for brushing each side of the prepared wontons.

6. Cook them in the air fryer for four minutes.

7. Serve hot.

Mushrooms and Steak

Total Prep & Cooking Time: Four hours and fifty minutes

Yields: Forty servings

Nutrition Facts: Calories: 220 | Protein: 19.1g | Carbs: 5.7g | Fat: 12g | Fiber: 0.7g

Ingredients

- One pound of beef sirloin steak (cut in cubes of one inch)
- Eight ounces of button mushrooms (sliced)
- One-fourth cup of Worcestershire sauce
- One tbsp. of olive oil
- One tsp. of parsley flakes
- Half tsp. of paprika
- One-third tsp. of chili flakes (crushed)

Method:

1. Mix mushrooms, steak, olive oil, Worcestershire sauce, paprika, parsley, and chili flakes in a mixing bowl. Refrigerate the mixture for four hours.
2. Take out the mixture thirty minutes prior to your cooking.
3. Preheat your air fryer at a temperature of 200 degrees Celsius.
4. Drain all the marinade. Place the mushrooms and steak into the air fryer basket.
5. Cook for five minutes. Toss the mixture and cook again for five minutes.

Rib Eye Steak

Total Prep & Cooking Time: Two hours and twenty-five minutes

Yields: Two servings

Nutrition Facts: Calories: 650 | Protein: 41.3g | Carbs: 7.2g | Fat: 48.1g | Fiber: 0.9g

Ingredients

- Two rib-eye steaks
- Four tsps. of grill seasoning
- One-fourth cup of olive oil
- Half cup soy sauce

Method:

1. Mix soy sauce, steak, seasoning, and olive oil in a large bowl. Marinate the steaks for two hours.
2. Add one tbsp. of water to the base of the basket for preventing smoking at the time of cooking.
3. Preheat to 200 degrees Celsius.
4. Add the marinated steaks and cook for seven minutes. Flip the steaks and cook again for seven minutes.
5. Let the steaks it for five minutes.
6. Serve warm.

Meatloaf

Total Prep & Cooking Time: Forty-five minutes

Yields: Forty servings

Nutrition Facts: Calories: 290 | Protein: 23.8g | Carbs: 5.6g | Fat: 17.6g | Fiber: 0.9g

Ingredients

- One pound of lean beef (ground)
- One large egg (beaten)
- Three tbsps. of bread crumbs
- One onion (chopped)

- One tbsp. of thyme (chopped)
- One tsp. of salt
- Half tsp. of black pepper (ground)
- Two mushrooms (sliced thick)
- Half tbsp. of olive oil

Method:

1. Start by preheating the air fryer at 200 degrees Celsius.
2. Mix egg, beef, bread crumbs, thyme, onion, pepper, and salt together in a bowl. Mix well.
3. Transfer the mixture of beef to the basket and use a spatula for smoothening the top. Take the mushrooms and press them at the top. Coat the loaf with some olive oil.
4. Set the timer to twenty-five minutes.
5. Let the meatloaf sit for ten minutes.
6. Slice in wedges and serve.

Fish Sticks

Total Prep & Cooking Time: Twenty minutes

Yields: Forty servings

Nutrition Facts: Calories: 183.2 | Protein: 25.6g | Carbs: 15.2g | Fat: 4.4g | Fiber: 0.9g

Ingredients

- One pound of cod fillets
- One-fourth cup of flour
- One large egg
- Half cup of bread crumbs
- One cup of parmesan cheese (grated)
- One tbsp. of parsley flakes
- One tsp. of paprika
- Half tsp. of black pepper (ground)
- One serving of cooking spray

Method:

1. Start by preheating your air fryer at 200 degrees Celsius.
2. Use paper towels for pat drying the fillets of fish. Cut the fillets into sticks of half an inch.
3. Add flour in a flat dish.

4. Break the egg and beat in a separate bowl.

5. Combine cheese, bread crumbs, paprika, parsley, and pepper in another dish.

6. Coat the fish sticks in flour and then dip in egg. Coat the sticks with bread crumb mixture.

7. Use a cooking spray for greasing the basket of the air fryer. Arrange the fish stick in the basket.

8. Cook for five minutes. Turn the sticks and cook again for five minutes.

9. Serve hot.

Cajun Salmon

Total Prep & Cooking Time: Twenty minutes

Yields: Two servings

Nutrition Facts: Calories: 321 | Protein: 31.7g | Carbs: 4.2g | Fat: 17.2g | Fiber: 0.6g

Ingredients

- Two fillets of salmon
- One serving of cooking spray
- One tbsp. of Cajun seasoning
- One tsp. of brown sugar

Method:

1. Dry the fish fillets using paper towels.
2. Use a cooking spray for misting the fillets.
3. Mix Cajun seasoning along with brown sugar in a bowl. Transfer the mixture into a flat dish.
4. Press the fillets of fish into the mixture of spices.
5. Spray the air fryer basket with cooking spray. Place the fillets with the skin-side down.
6. Cook the fish for eight minutes.
7. Let the fish sit for two minutes.
8. Serve hot.

Salmon Cakes and Sriracha Mayo

Total Prep & Cooking Time: Forty minutes

Yields: Four servings

Nutrition Facts: Calories: 329 | Protein: 24.3g | Carbs: 3.5g | Fat: 23.2g | Fiber: 2.5g

Ingredients

For sriracha mayo:

- One tbsp. of sriracha
- One-fourth cup of mayonnaise

For salmon cakes:

- One pound fillets of salmon (cut in pieces of one inch)
- One-third cup of almond flour
- One large egg (beaten)
- Two tsps. of seafood seasoning
- One green onion (chopped)
- One serving of cooking spray

Method:

1. Mix sriracha and mayonnaise in a bowl. Reserve one tbsp. of the mayo and refrigerate the rest.

2. Add almond flour, salmon, one and a half tsps. of seafood seasoning, egg, reserve sriracha mayo, and green onion to a food processor. Pulse the ingredients for five minutes.

3. Line a dish with parchment paper. Make eight patties from the mixture of fish. Chill the patties in the refrigerator for ten minutes.

4. Preheat your air fryer at 200 degrees Celsius. Use a cooking spray for greasing the basket.

5. Mist the patties with cooking spray and place them in the basket.

6. Cook for eight minutes.

7. Serve the salmon cakes with sriracha mayo by the side.

Cod With Sesame Crust and Snap Peas

Total Prep & Cooking Time: Thirty minutes

Yields: Four servings

Nutrition Facts: Calories: 356 | Protein: 30.2g | Carbs: 21.3g | Fat: 14.1g | Fiber: 7.2g

Ingredients

- Four fillets of cod
- One pinch of black pepper and salt
- Three tbsps. of butter (melted)
- Two tbsps. of sesame seeds
- One tbsp. of vegetable oil
- Two packs of snap peas
- Three garlic cloves (sliced thinly)
- One orange (cut in wedges)

Method:

1. Use vegetable oil for brushing the basket of the air fryer. Preheat at 200 degrees Celsius.
2. Sprinkle the fillets of cod with some pepper and salt.
3. Mix sesame seeds and butter in a bowl.
4. Toss garlic and peas with some butter.
5. Cook the peas in the air fryer for ten minutes.
6. Brush the fillets of fish with the mixture of butter and cook for four minutes. Flip the fillets and brush with the remaining butter mixture. Cook again for five minutes.
7. Serve the fish fillets with orange wedges and snap peas.

Grilled Fish and Pesto Sauce

Total Prep & Cooking Time: Twenty minutes

Yields: Two servings

Nutrition Facts: Calories: 1012 | Protein: 44.3g | Carbs: 3.2g | Fat: 93g | Fiber: 2.1g

Ingredients

- Two fillets of white fish
- One tsp. of olive oil
- Half tsp. of each
    - Black pepper (ground)
    - Salt

For the pesto sauce:

- One bunch of basil
- Two cloves of garlic
- One tbsp. of pine nuts
- Two tbsps. of parmesan cheese (grated)
- One cup of olive oil (extra virgin)

Method:

1. Heat your air fryer at 180 degrees Celsius.
2. Brush the fillets of fish with some oil. Sprinkle salt and pepper.
3. Cook the fish fillets for eight minutes.
4. Add garlic, basil leaves, cheese, pine nuts, and olive oil in a blender. Pulse the ingredients until a thick sauce forms.
5. Serve the fish fillets with pesto sauce from the top.

Chapter 3: Vegetarian Party Recipes

Besides cooking meat in an air fryer, you can also cook various vegetarian dishes with its help. In this section, you will find some tasty vegetarian dishes that you can make with the help of an air fryer.

Apple Pies

Total Prep & Cooking Time: Forty-five minutes

Yields: Four servings

Nutrition Facts: Calories: 476 | Protein: 3.3g | Carbs: 58.7g | Fat: 27.6g | Fiber: 3.6g

Ingredients

- Four tbsps. of butter
- Six tbsps. of brown sugar
- One tsp. of cinnamon (ground)
- Two apples (diced)
- Half tsp. of cornstarch
- Two tsps. of cold water
- Half package of pastry
- One serving of cooking spray
- Half tbsp. of grapeseed oil
- One-fourth cup of powdered sugar
- One tsp. of milk

Method:

1. Mix butter, apples, brown sugar, and ground cinnamon in a bowl. Add the mixture to a skillet and cook for five minutes until the apples are soft.

2. Combine cornstarch in water. Add the cornstarch mixture to the skillet.

3. Cook for one minute and keep aside.

4. Unroll the pastry crust and roll it out on a work surface with some flour. Cut the flattened dough in rectangles.

5. Place some apple filling at the center of each rectangle and fold the rectangles for sealing the pie.

6. Use a sharp knife for cutting small slits at the top.

7. Brush some oil at the top and cook for eight minutes at 195 degrees Celsius.

8. Combine milk and sugar in a bowl.

9. Serve the warm pies with sugar glaze from the top.

Fruit Crumble

Total Prep & Cooking Time: Thirty minutes

Yields: Two servings

Nutrition Facts: Calories: 308 | Protein: 2.3g | Carbs: 47.9g | Fat: 7.2g | Fiber: 5.3g

Ingredients

- One medium-sized apple
- Half cup of blueberries (frozen)
- One-fourth cup of brown rice flour
- Two tbsps. of sugar
- Half tsp. of cinnamon (ground)
- Three tbsps. of butter

Method:

1. Preheat your air fryer for five minutes at 170 degrees Celsius.
2. Mix blueberries and apple in a bowl.
3. Take a bowl and mix sugar, flour, butter, and cinnamon.
4. Pour the mixture of flour over the mixture of fruits.
5. Cook the fruits in the air fryer for fifteen minutes at 170 degrees Celsius.

Kiwi Chips

Total Prep & Cooking Time: One hour

Yields: Six servings

Nutrition Facts: Calories: 110 | Protein: 2.1g | Carbs: 26.3g | Fat: 1.1g | Fiber: 1.3g

Ingredients

- One kg of kiwi
- Half tsp. of cinnamon (ground)
- One-fourth tsp. of nutmeg (ground)

Method:

1. Slice the kiwi thinly. Keep them in a bowl.
2. Sprinkle nutmeg and cinnamon from the top. Toss for mixing.
3. Preheat the air fryer at 165 degrees Celsius.
4. Cook the kiwi in the air fryer for half an hour. Make sure you shake the basket halfway.
5. Let the chips cool down in the basket for fifteen minutes.
6. Cool before serving.

Apple Crisp

Total Prep & Cooking Time: Twenty-five minutes

Yields: Two servings

Nutrition Facts: Calories: 341 | Protein: 3.9g | Carbs: 60.5g | Fat: 12.3g | Fiber: 6.9g

Ingredients

- Two apples (chopped)
- One tsp. of each
    - Lemon juice
    - Cinnamon
- Two tbsps. of brown sugar

For the topping:

- Three tbsps. of flour
- Two tbsps. of brown sugar
- Half tsp. of salt
- Four tbsps. of rolled oats
- One and a half tbsps. of butter

Method:

1. Heat your air fryer at 170 degrees Celsius. Use butter for greasing the basket.

2. Combine lemon juice, apples, cinnamon, and sugar together in a bowl.

3. Cook the mixture for fifteen minutes. Shake the basket and cook again for five minutes.

4. For the topping, mix sugar, flour, salt, butter, and oats. Use an electric mixer for mixing.

5. Scatter the topping over the cooked apples.

6. Return the basket to the air fryer. Cook again for five minutes.

Roasted Veggies

Total Prep & Cooking Time: Thirty minutes

Yields: Four servings

Nutrition Facts: Calories: 35 | Protein: 1.3g | Carbs: 3.3g | Fat: 2.6g | Fiber: 1.6g

Ingredients

- Half cup of each
    - Summer squash (diced)
    - Zucchini (diced)
    - Mushrooms (diced)
    - Cauliflower (diced)
    - Asparagus (diced)
    - Sweet red pepper (diced)
- Two tsps. of vegetable oil
- One-fourth tsp. of salt
- Half tsp. of black pepper (ground)
- One tsp. of seasoning

Method:

1. Preheat air fryer at 180 degrees Celsius.
2. Mix all the veggies, oil, pepper, seasoning, and salt in a bowl. Toss well for coating.
3. Cook the mixture of veggies in the air fryer for ten minutes.

Tempura Vegetables

Total Prep & Cooking Time: Thirty-five minutes

Yields: Four servings

Nutrition Facts: Calories: 242 | Protein: 9.2g | Carbs: 35.6g | Fat: 9.3g | Fiber: 3.7g

Ingredients

- Half cup of each
    - Flour
    - Green beans
    - Onion rings

- Asparagus spears
- Sweet pepper rings
- Zucchini slices
- Avocado wedges
- Half tsp. of each
  - Black pepper (ground)
  - Salt
- Two large eggs
- Two tbsps. of water
- One cup of panko bread crumbs
- Two tsps. of vegetable oil

Method:

1. Combine flour, pepper, and one-fourth tsp. of salt in a dish.
2. Combine water and eggs in a shallow dish.
3. Mix oil and bread crumbs in another shallow dish.
4. Sprinkle remaining salt over the veggies.
5. Dip the veggies in the mixture of flour, then in the mixture of egg, and then coat in bread crumbs.
6. Cook the veggies in the air fryer for ten minutes. Shake in between.

Eggplant Parmesan

Total Prep & Cooking Time: Thirty-five minutes

Yields: Four servings

Nutrition Facts: Calories: 370 | Protein: 24g | Carbs: 35.6g | Fat: 17g | Fiber: 8.6g

Ingredients

- Half cup of bread crumbs (Italian)
- One-fourth cup of parmesan cheese (grated)
- One tsp. of each
    - Salt
    - Italian seasoning
- Half tsp. of each
    - Basil (dried)
    - Garlic powder
    - Onion powder
    - Black pepper (ground)
- One cup of flour
- Two large eggs (beaten)
- One eggplant (sliced in round of half an inch)
- One-third cup of marinara sauce
- Eight slices of mozzarella cheese

Method:

1. Mix parmesan cheese, bread crumbs, seasoning, basil, salt, onion powder, garlic powder, and black pepper together in a mixing bowl.

2. Add flour in a shallow dish.

3. Beat the eggs in a bowl.

4. Dip the slices of eggplants in flour and then in eggs. Coat the eggplants in the mixture of bread crumbs.

5. Cook the eggplants in the air fryer for ten minutes. Flip and cook for four minutes.

6. Top the slices of eggplants with one slice of mozzarella cheese and marinara sauce.

7. Cook again for two minutes.

8. Serve hot.

French Fries

Total Prep & Cooking Time: One hour

Yields: Four servings

Nutrition Facts: Calories: 108 | Protein: 2.4g | Carbs: 17.9g | Fat: 2.1g | Fiber: 3.2g

Ingredients

- One pound of russet potatoes (peeled)
- Two tsps. of vegetable oil

- One pinch of cayenne pepper
- Half tsp. of salt

Method:

1. Cut the potatoes in half-inch slices lengthwise.
2. Soak the potatoes in water for five minutes.
3. Drain the water and soak again in boiling water for ten minutes.
4. Drain all the water. Pat dry using paper towels.
5. Add oil and cayenne pepper. Season with salt.
6. Cook the potatoes for fifteen minutes. Toss with some salt and cook again for five minutes.

Sweet and Spicy Carrots

Total Prep & Cooking Time: Thirty minutes

Yields: Two servings

Nutrition Facts: Calories: 128 | Protein: 1.2g | Carbs: 17.2g | Fat: 6g | Fiber: 4.5g

Ingredients

- One serving of cooking spray
- One tbsp. of each
    - Hot honey
    - Butter (melted)
    - Orange zest
    - Orange juice
- Half tsp. of cardamom (ground)
- Half pound of baby carrots
- One-third tsp. of black pepper and salt

Method:

1. Heat your air fryer at 200 degrees Celsius. Use a cooking spray for greasing the basket.
2. Mix honey, butter, cardamom, and orange zest in a small bowl.
3. Pour the sauce over the carrots and coat well.
4. Cook the carrots for seven twenty minutes. Toss in between.
5. Mix orange juice with the leftover sauce.
6. Serve the carrots with sauce from the top.

Baked Potatoes

Total Prep & Cooking Time: One hour and five minutes

Yields: Two servings

Nutrition Facts: Calories: 310 | Protein: 7.2g | Carbs: 61.5g | Fat: 6.3g | Fiber: 8.2g

Ingredients

- Two large potatoes
- One tbsp. of peanut oil
- Half tsp. of sea salt

Method:

1. Heat your air fryer at 200 degrees Celsius.
2. Brush the potatoes with oil. Sprinkle some salt.
3. Place the potatoes in the basket of the air fryer and cook for one hour.
4. Serve hot by dividing the potatoes from the center.

Chapter 4: Vegetarian Appetizer Recipes

You can prepare various vegetarian appetizer recipes with the help of an air fryer. Let's have a look at them.

Crunchy Brussels Sprouts

Total Prep & Cooking Time: Fifteen minutes

Yields: Two servings

Nutrition Facts: Calories: 92 | Protein: 5.2g | Carbs: 12.1g | Fat: 3.1g | Fiber: 3.2g

Ingredients

- One tsp. of avocado oil
- Half tsp. of each
    - Black pepper (ground)
    - Salt
- Ten ounces of Brussels sprouts (halved)
- One-third tsp. of balsamic vinegar

Method:

1. Heat the air fryer at 175 degrees Celsius.
2. Mix salt, pepper, and oil together in a bowl. Add the sprouts and toss.
3. Fry the Brussels sprouts in the air fryer for five minutes.

Buffalo Cauliflower

Total Prep & Cooking Time: Twenty-five minutes

Yields: Four servings

Nutrition Facts: Calories: 190 | Protein: 12.3g | Carbs: 2.3g | Fat: 12g | Fiber: 1.3g

Ingredients

- One large cauliflower
- One cup of flour
- One-fourth tsp. of each
    - Chili powder
    - Cayenne pepper
    - Paprika
- One cup of soy milk
- Two tbsps. of butter
- Two garlic cloves (minced)
- Half cup of cayenne pepper sauce
- One serving of cooking spray

Method:

1. Cut the cauliflower into small pieces. Rinse under cold water and drain.

2. Mix flour, chili powder, cayenne, and paprika in a bowl. Add the milk slowly for making a thick batter.

3. Add the pieces of cauliflower in the batter and coat well.

4. Cook the cauliflower in the air fryer for twenty minutes. Toss the cauliflower and cook again for ten minutes.

5. Take a saucepan and heat the butter in it. Add garlic and hot sauce. Boil the sauce mixture and simmer for two minutes.

6. Transfer the cauliflower to a large bowl and pour the prepared sauce over the cooked cauliflower. Toss for combining.

7. Serve hot.

Stuffed Mushrooms

Total Prep & Cooking Time: Thirty minutes

Yields: Six servings

Nutrition Facts: Calories: 42 | Protein: 3.1g | Carbs: 2.9g | Fat: 1.2g | Fiber: 2.3g

Ingredients

- Fifteen button mushrooms
- One tsp. of olive oil
- One-eighth tsp. of salt
- Half tsp. of black pepper (crushed)
- One-third tsp. of balsamic vinegar

For the filling:

- One-fourth cup of each
    - Bell pepper
    - Onion
- Two tbsps. of cilantro (chopped)
- One tbsp. of jalapeno (chopped finely)
- Half cup of mozzarella cheese (grated)
- One tsp. of coriander (ground)
- One-fourth tsp. of each
    - Paprika
    - Salt

Method:

1. Use a damp cloth for cleaning the mushrooms. Remove the stems for making the caps hollow.

2. Take a bowl and season the mushroom caps with salt, oil, balsamic vinegar, and black pepper.

3. Take another bowl and mix the ingredients for the filling.

4. Use a spoon for filling the mushroom caps. Press the filling in the mushroom using the backside of the spoon.

5. Cook the mushrooms in the air fryer for ten minutes.

6. Serve hot.

Sweet Potatoes With Baked Taquitos

Total Prep & Cooking Time: Forty-five minutes

Yields: Five servings

Nutrition Facts: Calories: 112 | Protein: 5.2g | Carbs: 19.3g | Fat: 1.6g | Fiber: 6.1g

Ingredients

- One sweet potato (cut in pieces of half an inch)
- Two tsps. of canola oil
- Half cup yellow onion (chopped)
- One garlic clove (minced)
- Two cups of black beans (rinsed)
- One chipotle pepper (chopped)

- Half tsp. of each
    - Paprika
    - Cumin
    - Chili powder
    - Maple syrup
- One-eighth tsp. of salt
- Three tbsps. of water
- Ten corn tortillas

Method:

1. Place the pieces of sweet potatoes in an air fryer and toss it with some oil. Cook for twelve minutes. Make sure you shake the basket in between.

2. Take a skillet and heat some oil in it. Add the garlic and onions. Sauté for five minutes until the onions are translucent.

3. Add chipotle pepper, beans, paprika, cumin, chili powder, maple syrup, and salt. Add two tbsps. of water and mix all the ingredients.

4. Add cooked potatoes and mix well.

5. Warm the corn tortillas in a skillet.

6. Put two tbsps. of beans and potato mixture in a row across the corn tortillas. Grab one end of the corn tortillas and roll them. Tuck the end under the mixture of sweet potato and beans.

7. Place the taquitos with the seam side down in the basket. Spray the taquitos with some oil. Air fry the prepared taquitos for ten minutes.

8. Serve hot.

Cauliflower Curry

Total Prep & Cooking Time: Twenty minutes

Yields: Three servings

Nutrition Facts: Calories: 160 | Protein: 5.2g | Carbs: 27.2g | Fat: 3.1g | Fiber: 5.6g

Ingredients

- One cup of vegetable stock
- Three-fourth cup of coconut milk (light)
- Two tsps. of curry powder
- One tsp. of garlic puree
- Half tsp. of turmeric
- Twelve ounces of cauliflower (cut in florets)
- One and a half cup of sweet corn kernels
- Three spring onions (sliced)
- Salt

For the topping:

- Lime wedges
- Two tbsps. of dried cranberries

Method

1. Heat your air fryer at 190 degrees Celsius.
2. Mix all ingredients in a large bowl. Combine well.
3. Transfer the cauliflower mixture to the air fryer basket.
4. Cook for fifteen minutes. Give it a mix in the middle.

Air-Fried Avocado Wedges

Total Prep & Cooking Time: Twenty minutes

Yields: Two servings

Nutrition Facts: Calories: 302 | Protein: 8.3g | Carbs: 37.2g | Fat: 17.3g | Fiber: 7.4g

Ingredients

- One-fourth cup of flour
- Half tsp. of black pepper (ground)
- One-fourth tsp. of salt
- One tsp. of water
- One ripe avocado (cut in eight slices)
- Half cup of bread crumbs
- One serving of cooking spray

Method:

1. Heat your air fryer at 200 degrees Celsius.
2. Combine pepper, salt, and flour in a bowl. Place water in another bowl.
3. Take a shallow dish and spread the bread crumbs.
4. Coat the avocado slices in flour mixture and dip it in water.
5. Coat the slices in bread crumbs. Make sure both sides are evenly coated.
6. Use cooking spray for misting the slices of avocado.
7. Cook the coated slices of avocado for four minutes. Flip the slices and cook again for three minutes.
8. Serve hot.

Crunchy Grains

Total Prep & Cooking Time: Twenty minutes

Yields: Four servings

Nutrition Facts: Calories: 71 | Protein: 5.8g | Carbs: 34.4g | Fat: 3.2g | Fiber: 7.3g

Ingredients

- Three cups of whole grains (cooked)
- Half cup of peanut oil

Method:

1. Use a paper towel for removing excess moisture from the grains.
2. Toss the grains in oil.
3. Add the coated grains in the basket of the air fryer. Cook for ten minutes. Toss the grains and cook again for five minutes.

Buffalo Chickpeas

Total Prep & Cooking Time: Thirty minutes

Yields: Two servings

Nutrition Facts: Calories: 172 | Protein: 7.2g | Carbs: 31.6g | Fat: 1.4g | Fiber: 7.4g

Ingredients

- One can of chickpeas (rinsed)
- Two tbsps. of buffalo wing sauce
- One tbsp. of ranch dressing mix (dry)

Method:

1. Heat your air fryer at 175 degrees Celsius.
2. Use paper towels for removing excess moisture from the chickpeas.
3. Transfer the chickpeas to a bowl and add the wing sauce. Add the dressing mix and combine well.
4. Cook the chickpeas in the air fryer for eight minutes. Shake the basket and cook for five minutes.
5. Let the chickpeas sit for two minutes.
6. Serve warm.

Easy Falafel

Total Prep & Cooking Time: Forty minutes

Yields: Fifteen servings

Nutrition Facts: Calories: 57.9 | Protein: 3.2g | Carbs: 8.9g | Fat: 1.4g | Fiber: 3.9g

Ingredients

- One cup of garbanzo beans
- Two cups of cilantro (remove the stems)
- Three-fourth cup of parsley (remove the stems)
- On red onion (quartered)
- One garlic clove
- Two tbsps. of chickpea flour
- One tbsp. of each
    - Cumin (ground)
    - Coriander (ground)
    - Sriracha sauce
- One tsp. of black pepper and salt (for seasoning)
- Half tsp. of each
    - Baking soda
    - Baking powder
- One serving of cooking spray

Method:

1. Soak the beans in cool water for one day. Rub the beans and remove the skin. Rinse in cold water and use paper towels for removing excess moisture.

2. Add cilantro, beans, onion, parsley, and garlic in a blender. Blend the ingredients until paste forms.

3. Transfer the blended paste to a bowl and add coriander, flour, sriracha, cumin, pepper, and salt. Mix well. Let the mixture sit for twenty minutes.

4. Add baking soda and baking powder to the mixture. Mix well.

5. Make fifteen balls from the mixture and flatten them using your hands for making patties.

6. Usea cooking spray for greasing the falafel patties.

7. Cook them for ten minutes.

8. Serve warm.

Mini Cheese and Bean Tacos

Total Prep & Cooking Time: Thirty minutes

Yields: Twelve servings

Nutrition Facts: Calories: 229 | Protein: 11.3g | Carbs: 20.2g | Fat: 10.4g | Fiber: 2.9g

Ingredients

- One can of refried beans
- One ounce of taco seasoning mix
- Twelve slices of American cheese (halved)
- Twelve tortillas
- One serving of cooking spray

Method:

1. Place the beans in a medium-sized bowl. Add the seasoning mix. Combine well.

2. Place one cheese piece in the center of each tortilla. Take one tbsp. of the bean mix and add it over the cheese. Add another cheese piece over the beans. Fold the tortillas in half. Gently press with your hands for sealing the ends.

3. Use cooking spray for spraying the tacos.

4. Cook the tacos for three minutes. Turn the tacos and cook again for three minutes.

5. Serve hot.

Green Beans and Spicy Sauce

Total Prep & Cooking Time: Thirty minutes

Yields: Four servings

Nutrition Facts: Calories: 460.2 | Protein: 5.7g | Carbs: 34.4g | Fat: 30.6g | Fiber: 4.2g

Ingredients

- One cup of beer
- One and a half cup of flour
- Two tsps. of salt

- Half tsp. of black pepper (ground)
- Twelve ounces of green beans (trimmed)

For the sauce:

- One cup of ranch dressing
- Two tsps. of sriracha sauce
- One tsp. of horseradish

Method:

1. Mix flour, beer, pepper, and salt in a mixing bowl. Add the beans in the batter and coat well. Shake off extra batter.

2. Line the air fryer basket with parchment paper. Add the beans and cook for ten minutes. Shake in between.

3. Combine sriracha sauce, ranch dressing, and horseradish together in a bowl.

4. Serve the beans with sauce by the side.

Cheesy Sugar Snap Peas

Total Prep & Cooking Time: Fifteen minutes

Yields: Four servings

Nutrition Facts: Calories: 72 | Protein: 5.7g | Carbs: 8.9g | Fat: 3.3g | Fiber: 2.5g

Ingredients

- Half pound of sugar snap peas
- One tsp. of olive oil
- One-fourth cup of bread crumbs
- Half cup of parmesan cheese
- Pepper and salt (for seasoning)
- Two tbsps. of garlic (minced)

Method:

1. Remove the stem from each pea pod. Rinse the peas and drain the water.
2. Toss the peas with bread crumbs, olive oil, pepper, salt, and half of the cheese.
3. Cook the peas in the air fryer for four minutes at 175 degrees Celsius.
4. Add minced garlic and cook again for five minutes.
5. Serve the peas with remaining cheese from the top.

PART III

Vegan Cookbook

The vegan diet has gained immense popularity in the past few years. With an increasing number of participants, people have made up their mind to opt for the vegan options for health, environmental, or ethical reasons. When done in the perfect way, a vegan diet can help in showcasing a wide array of health benefits, for example, better control over blood sugar and a slimmer waistline. However, when a diet is based entirely on plant derivatives, it can result in a nutrient deficiency in various cases.

Veganism is being defined as a simple way of living that aims at excluding all major forms of animal cruelty and exploitation, whether for daily food, clothing, or some other purpose. For all these reasons, this diet does not include any form of animal products, such as eggs, dairy, and meat. It has been found that all those people who tend to practice veganism are thinner and also comes with a lower BMI or body mass index when compared with non-vegans. This can easily explain the primary reason why the majority of the people are turning to this form of diet as the only way for losing extra weight.

Adopting a vegan diet can help keep the blood sugar level under proper check and type 2 diabetes. According to some studies, vegans tend to benefit from the lower levels of blood sugar, higher sensitivity to insulin, and about 77% lower risk of developing diabetes than the non-vegans. The majority of the advantages can be easily explained by the increased consumption of fiber, which can blunt the blood sugar response. Several observational studies reported that vegans could have a 74% lower risk of having increased blood pressure along with a 43% lower risk of suffering from any chronic heart disease.

There is a specific food group that you will need to omit for following a vegan diet. This group of foods includes:

- **Poultry and meat:** Lamb, beef, veal, pork, organ meat, chicken, wild meat, goose, turkey, duck, etc.
- **Dairy:** Yogurt, butter, milk, cheese, ice cream, cream, etc.

- **Seafood and fish:** Fish of all types, squid, anchovies, calamari, shrimp, lobster, mussels, crab, etc.

- **Eggs:** From ostrich, chicken, fish, quail, etc.

- **Products from bees:** Bee pollen, honey, royal jelly, etc.

- **Ingredients based on animals:** Casein, whey, egg white albumen, shellac, lactose, gelatin, L-cysteine, isinglass, omega-3 fatty acids derived from fish, vitamin D3 derived from animals, and carmine.

You can opt for alternatives such as legumes, seitan, tofu, seeds, nut butter, nuts, veggies, fruits, whole grains, etc. The cooking style will remain the same, and the only difference will be the ingredients you are going to use.

Chapter 1: Breakfast Recipes

Breakfast is an essential meal of the day that needs to be fulfilled properly. Here are some vegan breakfast recipes for you.

Shamrock Sandwich

Total Prep & Cooking Time: Fifteen minutes

Yields: One serving

Nutrition Facts: Calories: 562 | Protein: 23g | Carbs: 43.2g | Fat: 31g | Fiber: 8.3g

Ingredients:

- One sausage patty (vegan)
- One cup of kale
- Two tsps. of olive oil (extra virgin)
- One tbsp. of pepitas
- Pepper and salt (according to taste)

For the sauce:

- One tbsp. of vegan mayonnaise
- One tsp. of jalapeno (chopped)
- One-fourth tsp. of paprika (smoky)

Other ingredients:

- One-fourth of an avocado (sliced)
- One toasted English muffin

Method:

1. Start by toasting the English muffin and keep it aside.
2. Take a sauté pan and drizzle some oil in it. Add the sausage patty and cook for two minutes on each side.
3. Add pepitas and kale to the hot pan. Add pepper and salt for adjusting the taste. When the kale gets soft, and the patty gets browned, remove the pan from heat.
4. Combine the spicy sauce.
5. Assemble the sandwich with sauce on the muffins and add the patty, avocado, pepitas, and kale.

Breakfast Burrito

Total Prep & Cooking Time: Thirty minutes

Yields: Two servings

Nutrition Facts: Calories: 618 | Protein: 20.3g | Carbs: 113g | Fat: 13.7g | Fiber: 21g

Ingredients:

- Three-fourth cup of rice (rinsed)
- Two cups of water
- One-fourth tsp. of salt
- One tbsp. of lime juice
- Half cup of cilantro (chopped)

For onions and hash browns:

- Half red onion
- Four red potatoes
- Two tbsp. of olive oil
- One-fourth tsp. of each
    - Black pepper (ground)
    - Salt

For black beans:

- One cup of black beans (cooked)
- One-fourth tsp. of each
    - Chili powder
    - Cumin powder
    - Garlic powder

For the avocado slaw:

- One avocado
- Two tbsps. of lime juice
- One cup of green cabbage (sliced thinly)
- One jalapeno (sliced)
- Half tsp. of each
    - Black pepper
    - Salt

For serving:

- Two flour tortillas
- Half avocado (ripe, sliced)
- One-fourth cup of salsa

Method:

1. Boil water, salt, and rice in a pan. Simmer the mixture for twenty minutes until the rice turns fluffy. Drain and keep aside.

2. Heat oil in a pan. Chop the potatoes into small pieces and slice the onions in rings. Add the potatoes along with the onions to the pan. Add pepper and salt for seasoning; toss the mixture for five minutes. Keep aside.

3. Prepare the beans in a saucepan over a medium flame.

4. For making the slaw, mix lime juice and avocado in a bowl. Mash the avocado and mix. Add jalapeno, cabbage, and toss for combining. Add pepper and salt for seasoning.

5. Add cilantro and lime juice to the rice and combine using a fork.

6. Warm the tortillas in a pan or microwave for twenty seconds.

7. Add the prepared fillings to the tortillas in order of your choice and top with salsa; add sliced avocado from the top. Roll the tortillas and slice in half.

8. Serve with extra black beans and potatoes by the side.

Gingerbread Waffles

Total Prep & Cooking Time: Fifteen minutes

Yields: Six servings

Nutrition Facts: Calories: 170 | Protein: 4.2g | Carbs: 27.3g | Fat: 4.7g | Fiber: 3.9g

Ingredients:

- One cup of flour
- One tbsp. of flax seeds (ground)

- Two tsps. of baking powder
- One-fourth tsp. of each
    - Salt
    - Baking soda
- One tsp. of cinnamon (ground)
- One and a half tsps. of ginger (ground)
- Four tbsps. of brown sugar
- One cup of any non-dairy milk
- Two tbsps. of apple cider vinegar
- Two tbsps. of molasses
- One and a half tbsps. of olive oil

Method:

1. Preheat a waffle iron and grease it.
2. Put the dry ingredients in a mixing bowl and combine well.
3. Combine the wet ingredients in a medium mixing bowl or jug. Mix well until properly combined.
4. Add the mixture of wet ingredients into the dry mixture and mix well. The batter needs to be thick. In case the batter is excessively thick, you can add two tbsps. of non-dairy milk to the batter and mix.
5. Pour the batter in batches in the waffle iron and cook until steam stops to come out from the sides.
6. Open the waffle iron and take out the waffle carefully.
7. Serve warm.

Green Chickpeas And Toast

Total Prep & Cooking Time: Thirty minutes

Yields: Two servings

Nutrition Facts: Calories: 189 | Protein: 11.3g | Carbs: 27.1g | Fat: 3.2g | Fiber: 9.3g

Ingredients:

- Two tbsps. of olive oil
- Three shallots (diced)
- One-fourth tsp. of paprika (smoked)
- Two cloves of garlic (diced)
- Half tsp. of each
    - Sweet paprika
    - Salt
    - Cinnamon
    - Sugar
- Black pepper (according to taste)
- Two tomatoes (skinned)
- Two cups of chickpeas (cooked)
- Four crusty bread slices

Method:

1. Take a medium pan and heat oil in it.

2. Add the diced shallots to the oil and stir-fry. Add garlic to the pan. Cook for five minutes until shallots turn translucent.

3. Add spices to the pan and combine well with garlic and shallots. Stir for two minutes.

4. Add the tomatoes to the pan and squash them using a spoon or spatula. Add four tbsps. of water to the pan and simmer for twelve minutes.

5. Add cooked chickpeas and mix well. Add pepper, sugar, and salt.

6. Serve the cooked chickpeas on bread slices.

Asparagus And Tomato Quiche

Total Prep & Cooking Time: One hour and twenty minutes

Yields: Eight servings

Nutrition Facts: Calories: 219 | Protein: 4.1g | Carbs: 20.6g | Fat: 11.7g | Fiber: 3g

Ingredients:

- Two cups of flour
- Half tsp. of salt
- Half cup of non-dairy butter
- Two tbsps. of water (ice cold)

For filling:

- One tbsp. of coconut oil
- One cup of asparagus (chopped)
- One-fourth cup of onion (minced)
- Three tbsps. of each
    - Sun-dried tomatoes (chopped)
    - Nutritional yeast
    - Basil (chopped)
- One block of tofu (firm)
- One tbsp. of each
    - Flour
    - Non-dairy milk

- One tsp. of each
    - Minced onion (dehydrated)
    - Mustard
- Two tsps. of lemon juice
- Half tsp. of each
    - Salt
    - Turmeric
    - Liquid smoke

Method:

1. Spray a pie pan with oil and keep aside. Preheat your oven at 180 degrees Celsius.

2. Mix salt along with flour in a bowl. Add non-dairy butter along with cold water to the flour. Knead the dough on a working surface.

3. Press the dough on the pan. Bake the dough in the preheated oven for ten minutes.

4. Heat some oil in a pan and start adding asparagus, tomato, and onion. Cook for three minutes.

5. Combine onion, tofu, yeast, flour, non-dairy milk, lemon juice, liquid smoke, and salt in a blender.

6. Combine the mixture of asparagus with the tofu mixture.

7. Add the filling on the baked crust and smoothen the top.

8. Bake for half an hour.

9. Serve warm.

Breakfast Bowl

Total Prep & Cooking Time: One hour and twenty-five minutes

Yields: Two servings

Nutrition Facts: Calories: 350 | Protein: 7.2g | Carbs: 54g | Fat: 11.3g | Fiber: 9.3g

Ingredients:

- Two small sweet potatoes
- Cinnamon (ground, according to taste)
- Two tbsps. of each
    - Chopped nuts
    - Raisins
    - Almond butter

Method:

1. Preheat your oven at 180/160 degrees Celsius. Wash the potatoes and dry them using a kitchen towel. Use a fork for poking holes in the potatoes and wrap them using aluminum foil. Bake the potatoes for eighty minutes. Allow the potatoes to cool down before peeling.

2. Peel the baked potatoes and mash them with cinnamon.

3. Top with chopped nuts and raisins. Drizzle some almond butter from the top and serve.

Tofu Pancakes

Total Prep & Cooking Time: Twenty minutes

Yields: Six servings

Nutrition Facts: Calories: 370 | Protein: 11.2g | Carbs: 46.3g | Fat: 13.2g | Fiber: 7.9g

Ingredients:

- Fifty grams of Brazil nuts
- Three bananas (sliced)
- Three-hundred grams of raspberries
- Maple syrup (for serving)

For batter:

- Four-hundred grams of firm tofu
- Two tsps. of each
    - Lemon juice
    - Vanilla extract
- Four-hundred ml of almond milk
- One tbsp. of vegetable oil
- Two cups of buckwheat flour
- Four tbsps. of sugar
- Two tsps. of mixed spice (ground)
- One tbsp. of baking powder

Method:

1. Preheat your oven at 160 degrees Celsius. Cook the nuts by scattering them in a tray for five minutes. Chop the nuts.

2. Add vanilla, tofu, almond milk, and lemon juice in a deep bowl; blend the mixture using a stick blender. Add oil to the mixture and blend again.

3. Take a large bowl and combine the dry ingredients; add one tsp. of salt and combine. Add the mixture of tofu and combine.

4. Heat a pan and add one tsp. oil in it. Make sure that the pan is not excessively hot.

5. Use a large spoon for dropping three spoons of batter in the pan. Swirl the pan for making the pancake even—Cook for two minutes on each side. Repeat the same for the remaining batter.

6. Serve with berries, bananas, nuts, and drizzle some maple syrup from the top.

Chapter 2: Side Dish Recipes

Side dish plays a profound role in any proper meal. I have included some tasty and easy vegan side dish recipes in this section.

Baked Beans

Total Prep & Cooking Time: Five hours and twenty minutes

Yields: Ten servings

Nutrition Facts: Calories: 249 | Protein: 11.2g | Carbs: 45.3g | Fat: 2.9g | Fiber: 13.7g

Ingredients:

- Sixteen ounces of navy beans (dry)
- Six cups of water
- Two tbsps. of olive oil
- Two cups of sweet onion (chopped)
- One garlic clove (minced)
- Four cans of tomato sauce
- One-fourth cup of brown sugar
- Half cup of molasses
- Three tbsps. of cider vinegar
- Three bay leaves
- One tsp. of mustard (dry)
- One-fourth tsp. of each
    - Black pepper (ground)
    - Nutmeg (ground)
    - Cinnamon (ground)

Method:

1. Add water and beans in a pot and boil the mixture. Lower the flame and cook for one hour. Cook until the beans are tender. Drain the beans and keep aside.

2. Preheat your oven to 160 degrees Celsius.

3. Take an iron skillet and heat oil in it. Add onions in the oil. Cook for two minutes. Add garlic to the pan.

4. Combine the onion mixture with the cooked beans. Add tomato sauce, molasses, vinegar, brown sugar, pepper, bay leaves, cinnamon, mustard, and nutmeg. Mix well.

5. Cover the dish and bake for three hours. Stir in between.

6. Remove the cover and bake for forty minutes.

Baked Potato Wedges

Total Prep & Cooking Time: Fifty-five minutes

Yields: Four servings

Nutrition Facts: Calories: 234 | Protein: 5.1g | Carbs: 42.6g | Fat: 4.3g | Fiber: 8.9g

Ingredients:

- One tbsp. of olive oil
- Eight sweet potatoes (sliced into quarters)
- Half tsp. of paprika

Method:

1. Preheat your oven at 160/180 degrees Celsius.
2. Grease a baking sheet with cooking spray.
3. Combine potatoes and paprika in a bowl. Add the potatoes to the baking sheet.
4. Bake for forty minutes.
5. Serve warm.

Black Beans And Quinoa

Total Prep & Cooking Time: Fifty minutes

Yields: Ten servings

Nutrition Facts: Calories: 143 | Protein: 8.7g | Carbs: 25.6g | Fat: 1.2g | Fiber: 8.7g

Ingredients:

- One tsp. of vegetable oil
- One large onion (chopped)
- Three garlic cloves (chopped)
- Three-fourth cup of quinoa
- Two cups of vegetable stock
- One tsp. of cumin (ground)
- One-fourth tsp. of cayenne powder
- One cup of corn kernels (frozen)
- Two cans of black beans (rinsed)
- Half cup of cilantro (chopped)
- Pepper and salt (according to taste)

Method:

1. Take a medium pan and heat oil in it. Add garlic and onion to the pan. Cook for ten minutes until browned.
2. Add quinoa to the pan and mix well. Cover the mixture with vegetable stock. Season with salt, pepper, and cayenne. Boil the mixture. Cover the pan and simmer for twenty minutes until quinoa gets tender.
3. Add the corn kernels to the pan and simmer for five minutes.
4. Add cilantro and black beans to the mixture.
5. Serve hot.

Roasted Lemon Garlic Broccoli

Total Prep & Cooking Time: Twenty-five minutes

Yields: Six servings

Nutrition Facts: Calories: 48.3 | Protein: 3g | Carbs: 6.9g | Fat: 1.8g | Fiber: 3g

Ingredients:

- Two heads of broccoli (separate the florets)
- Two tsps. of olive oil (extra virgin)
- One tsp. of salt
- Half tsp. of black pepper (ground)
- One garlic clove (minced)
- One-fourth tsp. of lemon juice

Method:

1. Preheat your oven at 180/200 degrees Celsius.
2. Toss the florets of broccoli with olive oil in a bowl. Add pepper, garlic, and salt. Spread the coated broccoli florets on a baking sheet.
3. Bake for twenty minutes.
4. Add lemon juice from the top and serve warm.

Spicy Tofu

Total Prep & Cooking Time: Twenty minutes

Yields: Four servings

Nutrition Facts: Calories: 305.2 | Protein: 20.1g | Carbs: 15.4g | Fat: 19.3g | Fiber: 5.2g

Ingredients:

- Three tbsps. of peanut oil
- One red onion (sliced)
- One pound of tofu (firm, cubed)
- One bell pepper (sliced)
- One chili pepper (chopped)
- Three garlic cloves (crushed)
- One-third cup of hot water
- Two tbsps. of each
    - Soy sauce
    - White vinegar
- One tsp. of cornstarch
- One tbsp. of each
    - Red pepper flakes (crushed)
    - Brown sugar

Method:

1. Take a wok and heat oil in it. Add the tofu to the oil and keep cooking until browned. Add bell pepper, onion, garlic, and chili pepper. Mix well and cook for five minutes.

2. Whisk vinegar, soy sauce, red pepper flakes, brown sugar, and cornstarch in a bowl.

3. Add the mixture of vinegar to the wok and toss well for coating. Simmer the mixture for five minutes.

4. Serve hot.

Spanish Rice

Total Prep & Cooking Time: Forty minutes

Yields: Four servings

Nutrition Facts: Calories: 267.2 | Protein: 4.7g | Carbs: 42.7g | Fat: 5.6g | Fiber: 3g

Ingredients:

- Two tbsps. of vegetable oil
- One cup of white rice (uncooked)
- One onion (chopped)
- Half bell pepper (chopped)
- Two cups of water
- One can of green chilies and diced tomatoes
- Two tsps. of chili powder
- One tsp. of salt

Method:

1. Take a deep skillet and heat oil in it. Add onion, rice, and bell pepper to the skillet. Sauté until onions are soft and rice gets browned.
2. Add tomatoes and water to the skillet. Add salt and chili powder.
3. Simmer the mixture for thirty minutes and cover the skillet.
4. Serve hot.

Pepper And Lemon Pasta

Total Prep & Cooking Time: Twenty minutes

Yields: Eight servings

Nutrition Facts: Calories: 232.8 | Protein: 8.5g | Carbs: 41g | Fat: 4.6g | Fiber: 3.6g

Ingredients:

- One pound of spaghetti
- Two tbsps. of olive oil
- One tbsp. of basil (dried)
- Three tbsps. of lemon juice
- Black pepper (ground, according to taste)

Method:

1. Take a large pot and boil water in it with light salt. Add the pasta to the pot and cook for ten minutes. Drain the pasta.

2. Combine lemon juice, black pepper, lemon juice, and basil in a bowl.

3. Add the lemon mixture to the cooked pasta and toss it properly.

4. Serve cold or hot.

Chapter 3: High Protein Recipes

The vegan diet is rich in proteins, as it is mainly composed of plant compounds. Here are some easy to make vegan high protein recipes for you.

Kale Salad With Spicy Tempeh Bits And Chickpeas

Total Prep & Cooking Time: Forty-five minutes

Yields: Four servings

Nutrition Facts: Calories: 473 | Protein: 25g | Carbs: 41g | Fat: 27.1g | Fiber: 17.3g

Ingredients:

- Eight ounces of tempeh
- One-fourth cup of vegetable oil
- One-fourth tsp. of salt
- Two tsps. of each
    - Garlic powder
    - Onion powder
    - Sweet paprika
- One tsp. of each
    - Lemon pepper
    - Chili powder
- One-eighth tsp. of cayenne powder

For salad:

- 400 grams of kale (chopped)
- One cup of carrots (shredded)
- One can of chickpeas
- Two tbsps. of sesame seeds

For dressing:

- Half cup of rice vinegar
- One-fourth cup of soy sauce
- Two tbsps. of sesame oil
- One tbsp. of ginger (grated)

Method:

1. Boil water with salt in a large pot. Blanch the kale for thirty seconds. Wash blanched kale under running water. Squeeze out excess water from kale and keep aside.

2. Preheat your oven to 180 degrees Celsius.

3. Mix all the spices for tempeh in a mixing bowl.

4. Cut tempeh into very thin slices.

5. Dip each tempeh slice in oil and arrange them on a baking sheet. Line the tray using parchment paper. Sprinkle the mix of spices from the top. Coat well.

6. Bake tempeh for twenty minutes until crispy and brown in color.

7. Take a large bowl and combine the listed ingredients for the salad.

8. Combine the ingredients of dressing in a jar and shake well.

9. Pour the dressing over the prepared salad. Toss well. Make sure the salad gets coated properly with the dressing.

10. Crumble the slices of tempeh over the salad.

Protein Bars

Total Prep & Cooking Time: One hour and twenty minutes

Yields: Ten servings

Nutrition Facts: Calories: 292 | Protein: 13g | Carbs: 37.9g | Fat: 9.6g | Fiber: 2.3g

Ingredients:

For crust:

- Two cups of oat flour
- Six apricots (dried)
- One-fourth cup of each
    - Brown rice syrup
    - Cocoa powder

For layer:

- One cup of oat flour
- Half cup of each
    - Vegan protein powder (chocolate)
    - Rolled oats
- One-fourth tsp. of salt
- Two tbsps. of each
    - Hemp seeds (hulled)

- - Chia seeds
- Half cup of almond butter
- One-fourth cup of any vegan sweetener
- One cup of coconut milk
- One tbsp. flax seeds (ground)

Method:

1. Combine all the ingredients for the crust in a blender. Keep the dough aside.

2. Take a large bowl and mix the dry ingredients for the next layer. You can use a fork for proper mixing.

3. Mix water and flax in a bowl and keep aside until it turns into a gel.

4. Add almond butter, sweetener, coconut milk, and flax gel to the mixture of dry ingredients. Use a fork for mixing properly.

5. Pour the mixture in a food processor and blend well for making it smooth.

6. Use parchment paper for lining a baking sheet. Add the crust to the sheet and press the crust out. Add the next layer on the crust and evenly spread it out.

7. Put the baking sheet in the freezer for one hour.

8. Serve by cutting bars of your desired size and shape.

Tofu And Spinach Scramble

Total Prep & Cooking Time: Thirty minutes

Yields: Two servings

Nutrition Facts: Calories: 319 | Protein: 22.1g | Carbs: 11.4g | Fat: 22g | Fiber: 6.5g

Ingredients:

- Fourteen ounces of tofu (firm, cut into cubes of half-inch)
- Half tsp. of turmeric (ground)
- Black pepper and kosher salt (to taste)
- One-eighth tsp. of cayenne powder (ground)
- Two tbsps. of olive oil (extra virgin)
- Three scallions (sliced)
- Five ounces of spinach (chopped)
- Two tsps. of lemon juice
- One cup of grape tomatoes (halved)
- Half cup of basil (chopped)

Method:

1. Mix turmeric, tofu, one-fourth tsp. of salt, cayenne, and half tsp. of black pepper in a bowl. Toss the ingredients for mixing properly.

2. Take a large skillet and heat oil in it; add the scallions and stir for about one minute. Add tofu mixture and cook for five minutes until the tofu gets browned.

3. Add lemon juice, spinach, and half tsp. of salt to the tofu. Cook for one minute until the spinach wilts. Add tomatoes and stir for one minute.

4. Remove the skillet from heat and add basil.

5. Serve hot.

Vegan Tacos

Total Prep & Cooking Time: Twenty minutes

Yields: Six servings

Nutrition Facts: Calories: 402 | Protein: 29g | Carbs: 71.2g | Fat: 5.4g | Fiber: 20.3g

Ingredients:

- One tsp. of vegetable oil

- Half onion (diced)
- Two tsps. of jalapeno (chopped)
- Twelve ounces of soy chorizo (remove the casing)
- Sixteen ounces of refried black beans
- Twelve tortillas (corn)
- Cilantro (chopped)

Method:

1. Take a skillet and heat oil in it. Add onion and jalapeno to the skillet—Cook for ten minutes. Add chorizo and cook for five minutes.

2. Take a small pan and cook the beans on low heat.

3. Arrange two tortillas for making six tacos in total.

4. Spread the beans on the tortillas; top the beans with the mixture of chorizo. Serve with cilantro from the top.

Grilled Tofu Steaks And Spinach Salad

Total Prep & Cooking Time: One hour

Yields: Two servings

Nutrition Facts: Calories: 154 | Protein: 22g | Carbs: 8g | Fat: 11.3g | Fiber: 9.3g

Ingredients:

For tofu steak:

- Half block of tofu (firm)
- One tbsp. of soy sauce
- One tsp. of each
    - Miso paste
    - Tomato paste
    - Olive oil
- Half tsp. of maple syrup
- One-fourth cup of breadcrumbs

For spinach salad:

- Two cups of baby spinach
- One tbsp. of each
    - Olive oil (extra virgin)
    - Pine nuts
    - Lemon juice
- Pinch of salt
- Pinch of black pepper (ground)

Method:

1. Cut the tofu block in half and squeeze out any excess water. Make sure you do not break the block of tofu. Use paper towels for drying the tofu.

2. Cut the tofu in size and shape of your choice.

3. Take a small mixing bowl and combine tomato paste, soy sauce, olive oil, sesame, miso paste, and maple syrup. Mix until the sauce is smooth.

4. Spread breadcrumbs in a shallow dish.

5. Dip the pieces of tofu in the prepared sauce and then coat them in breadcrumbs. Repeat for the remaining tofu.

6. Grease a grill pan with some olive oil. Add the tofu steaks and cook for fifteen minutes on each side. Cook until both sides are browned.

7. For the salad, mix the listed ingredients in a medium-sized mixing bowl. Toss the ingredients properly.

8. Serve the tofu steaks with spinach salad by the side.

Corn, Quinoa, And Edamame Salad

Total Prep & Cooking Time: Two hours and ten minutes

Yields: Four servings

Nutrition Facts: Calories: 130 | Protein: 18g | Carbs: 13g | Fat: 5.8g | Fiber: 3.1g

Ingredients:

- One cup of corn kernels (frozen)
- Two cups of shelled edamame
- Half cup of cooked quinoa
- One green onion (sliced)
- Half sweet bell pepper (diced)
- Two tbsps. of cilantro (chopped)
- One and a half tbsps. of olive oil
- One tbsp. of each
    - Lime juice
    - Lemon juice
- One-fourth tsp. of each
    - Salt
    - Thyme (dried)
    - Chili powder
    - Black pepper (ground)

Method:

1. Boil corn and edamame in water with a little bit of salt. Drain and keep aside.
2. Take a bowl and mix corn, edamame, quinoa, bell pepper, green onion, and cilantro.
3. Whisk together lemon juice, olive oil, lime juice, chili powder, salt, thyme, and black pepper in a small bowl.
4. Pour the dressing all over the salad. Mix well.
5. Chill in the refrigerator for two hours.

Lentil Soup

Total Prep & Cooking Time: Fifty-five minutes

Yields: Six servings

Nutrition Facts: Calories: 230 | Protein: 9.2g | Carbs: 31.2g | Fat: 8.6g | Fiber: 11.3g

Ingredients:

- Two tbsps. of olive oil (extra virgin)
- One onion (diced)

- Two carrots (diced)
- Two stalks of celery (diced)
- One bell pepper (diced)
- Three garlic cloves (minced)
- One tbsp. of cumin
- One-fourth tsp. of paprika
- One tsp. of oregano
- Two cups of tomatoes (diced)
- Two cans of green lentils (rinsed)
- Eight cups of vegetable stock
- Half tsp. of salt
- Cilantro (for garnishing)
- One ripe avocado (diced)

Method:

1. Heat some oil in a pot. Start adding bell pepper, onion, carrots, and celery to the pot. Sauté the veggies for five minutes until tender; add paprika, cumin, garlic, and oregano. Mix well.

2. Add chilies, tomatoes, stock, salt, and lentils; simmer the mixture for forty minutes. Add pepper and salt according to taste.

3. Serve with avocado and cilantro from the top.

Chapter 4: Dessert Recipes

Everyone loves to have some dessert after having their meals. Desserts can be vegan too. So in this section, I have included some tasty dessert recipes that you can make easily.

Chocolate Pudding

Total Prep & Cooking Time: Forty-five minutes

Yields: Two servings

Nutrition Facts: Calories: 265.1 | Protein: 8.3g | Carbs: 52.2g | Fat: 4.6g | Fiber: 4.9g

Ingredients:

- Three tbsps. of cornstarch
- Two tbsps. of water
- Two cups of soy milk
- One-fourth tsp. of vanilla extract
- One-fourth cup of white sugar
- One cup of cocoa powder

Method:

1. Take a small bowl and mix water and cornstarch for forming a fine paste.
2. Take a saucepan and heat it over medium flame. Add soy milk, sugar, vanilla, a mixture of cornstarch, and cocoa. Stir the mixture until it starts boiling. Keep cooking until the mixture gets thick.
3. Allow the pudding to cool for five minutes.
4. Chill in the fridge for twenty minutes.

Orange Cake

Total Prep & Cooking Time: Forty-five minutes

Yields: Sixteen servings

Nutrition Facts: Calories: 147.3 | Protein: 1.9g | Carbs: 21.6g | Fat: 6.3g | Fiber: 0.8g

Ingredients:

- One large-sized onion (peeled)
- Two cups of flour
- One cup of white sugar
- Half cup of vegetable oil
- One and a half tsps. of baking soda
- Half tsp. of salt

Method:

1. Preheat your oven to 190 degrees Celsius. Grease a baking pan with some oil.
2. Blend the orange in a food processor until it gets completely liquefied.
3. Combine orange juice, sugar, flour, vegetable oil, baking soda, and salt. Pour the cake batter into prepared baking pan.
4. Bake the cake for thirty minutes.

Notes:

- In case you do not want to make orange juice at home, you can use orange juice from the store.
- This cake can be converted into a plain cake by omitting orange juice and using soy milk along with rice milk.

Pumpkin Tofu Pie

Total Prep & Cooking Time: Two hours

Yields: Eight servings

Nutrition Facts: Calories: 229.3 | Protein: 4.7g | Carbs: 33.6g | Fat: 8.6g | Fiber: 3.7g

Ingredients

- Ten ounces of silken tofu (drained)
- One can of pumpkin puree
- Three-fourth cup of white sugar
- Half tsp. of salt
- One tsp. of cinnamon (ground)
- One-fourth tsp. of ginger (ground)
- One-eighth tsp. of cloves (ground)
- One pie crust (unbaked)

Method:

1. Preheat the oven at 220/230 degrees Celsius.
2. Add pumpkin puree, tofu, cinnamon, salt, sugar, clove, and ginger in a food processor. Blend the ingredients until smooth.
3. Pour over the blended mixture into the crust.
4. Bake the pie for fifteen minutes and then reduce the temperature to 175 degrees Celsius. Bake again for forty minutes.
5. Let the pie cool down.
6. Serve at room temperature.

Note: If you are allergic to certain ingredients, check the ingredients of the pie crust.

Vegan Brownie

Total Prep & Cooking Time: Fifty minutes

Yields: Sixteen servings

Nutrition Facts: Calories: 254.3 | Protein: 2.6g | Carbs: 38.3g | Fat: 13.6g | Fiber: 2.8g

Ingredients:

- Two cups of flour
- Two cups of white sugar
- Three-fourth cup of cocoa powder (unsweetened)
- One tsp. of baking powder
- Half tsp. of salt
- One cup of each
    - Vegetable oil
    - Water
- One and a half tsps. of vanilla extract

Method:

1. Preheat your oven at 160/175 degrees Celsius.

2. Take a large bowl and combine sugar, flour, cocoa powder, salt, and baking powder. Add vegetable oil, vanilla extract, and water to the mixture. Mix well for making a smooth batter.

3. Spread the brownie mix in a baking pan.

4. Bake the brownie for thirty minutes.

5. Allow the brownie to cool for ten minutes.

6. Cut in squares and serve.

Vegan Cupcake

Total Prep & Cooking Time: Twenty-five minutes

Yields: Eighteen servings

Nutrition Facts: Calories: 150.2 | Protein: 1.9g | Carbs: 21.6g | Fat: 6.3g | Fiber: 0.9g

Ingredients:

- One tbsp. of cider vinegar
- Two cups of almond milk
- Two and a half cups of flour
- One cup of white sugar
- Two tsps. of baking powder
- Half tsp. of each
    - Salt
    - Baking soda
    - Coconut oil (warmed)
- One and a half tsps. of vanilla extract

Method:

1. Preheat the oven at 160/175 degrees Celsius. Grease eighteen muffin cups using some oil.

2. Mix cider vinegar and almond milk in a bowl. Allow it to stand for five minutes until the mixture gets curdled.

3. Take a bowl and combine sugar, salt, baking powder, flour, and baking soda.

4. Take another bowl and combine coconut oil, vanilla, and almond milk mixture. Add this mixture to the mixture of dry ingredients.

5. Divide the batter into muffin cups—Bake for twenty minutes.

6. Allow the cupcakes to sit for ten minutes.

7. Serve with the desired frosting from the top.

Vanilla Cake

Total Prep & Cooking Time: Fifty minutes

Yields: Eight servings

Nutrition Facts: Calories: 277.9 | Protein: 3.5g | Carbs: 44.2g | Fat: 9.2g | Fiber: 0.9g

Ingredients:

- One cup of soy milk
- One tbsp. of apple cider vinegar
- One and a half cup of flour
- One cup of white sugar
- One tsp. of each
    - Baking powder
    - Baking soda
- Half tsp. of salt
- One-third cup of canola oil
- One-fourth tsp. of almond extract
- One tbsp. of vanilla extract
- One-fourth cup of water

Method:

1. Preheat your oven at about 160/175 degrees Celsius. Grease a baking pan with some oil.

2. Mix vinegar and soy milk in a large cup.

3. Combine sugar, flour, salt, baking soda, and baking powder in a bowl.

4. Add lemon juice, canola oil, vanilla extract, almond extract, and water to the mixture of soy milk. Stir the mixture of soy milk into the mixture of flour. Mix well until there is no lump.

5. Pour the cake batter in the baking dish.

6. Bake in the preheated oven for thirty-five minutes.

Miracle Fudge

Total Prep & Cooking Time: One hour and ten minutes

Yields: Twenty-four servings

Nutrition Facts: Calories: 77.3 | Protein: 0.9g | Carbs: 4.9g | Fat: 6.2g | Fiber: 1.2g

Ingredients:

- Half cup of cocoa (unsweetened)
- One cup of maple syrup
- One tsp. of vanilla extract
- One pinch of salt
- One-third cup of each
    - Chopped walnuts
    - Coconut oil (melted)
- One tsp. of cocoa powder (unsweetened, for dusting)

Method

1. Add half cup of cocoa powder in a bowl along with maple syrup; give it a stir. Add vanilla extract and salt. Add melted coconut oil and combine well.

2. Add walnuts in a pan and toast them for one minute.

3. Add the toasted walnuts to the fudge. Mix well.

4. Pour the mixture of fudge into a silicone mold. Smoothen the top.

5. Wrap the silicone mold using plastic wrap and put it in the freezer for thirty minutes. Take out the fudge pieces from the mold and dust with cocoa powder from the top.

6. Serve cold.

Chapter 5: Sauces & Dips Recipes

Sauces and dips are important components of any meal that can make the food tastier. Here are some vegan sauces and dips recipes for you.

Tomato Jam

Total Prep & Cooking Time: Forty-five minutes

Yields: One full cup

Nutrition Facts: Calories: 34 | Protein: 0.2g | Carbs: 8.6g | Fat: 0.1g | Fiber: 0.2g

Ingredients:

- Two pounds of plum tomatoes
- One-fourth cup of coconut sugar
- Half tsp. of salt
- One-fourth tsp. of paprika
- One tsp. of vinegar (white wine)
- Black pepper (to taste)

Method:

1. Take a large pot and boil water in it; add the tomatoes to the water and boil for one minute. Remove the tomatoes and put them in an ice-water bath.
2. Peel the blanched tomatoes and chop them.
3. Add chopped tomatoes in a pot over a medium flame. Add sugar and stir the mixture—Cook for ten minutes.
4. Add pepper, salt, and paprika. Simmer for ten minutes until the jam thickens.
5. Remove from heat and add white wine vinegar. Serve with crackers, burgers, toasts, etc.

Walnut Kale Pesto

Total Prep & Cooking Time: Thirty minutes

Yields: One small bowl

Nutrition Facts: Calories: 240 | Protein: 3.6g | Carbs: 2.6g | Fat: 22.3g | Fiber: 0.8g

Ingredients:

- Half bunch of kale (chopped)
- Half cup of walnuts (chopped)
- Two garlic cloves (minced)
- One-fourth cup of yeast
- One cup of olive oil
- Three tbsps. of lemon juice
- Pepper and salt (for seasoning)

Method:

1. Take a pot and boil water in it. Add kale to the pot with one tsp. of salt—Cook for five minutes.

2. Add kale, garlic, walnuts, olive oil, yeast, along with lemon juice in a food processor. Add pepper and salt according to your taste. Blend well.

Ranch Dressing

Total Prep & Cooking Time: Thirty minutes

Yields: One small bowl

Nutrition Facts: Calories: 92 | Protein: 0.1g | Carbs: 1g | Fat: 9.1g | Fiber: 0.4g

Ingredients:

- One cup of vegan mayo
- Half tsp. of each
    - Onion powder
    - Garlic powder
- One-fourth tsp. of black pepper (ground)
- Two tsps. of parsley (chopped)
- One tbsp. of dill (chopped)
- Half cup of soy milk (unsweetened)

Method:

1. Mix the listed ingredients in a medium mixing bowl.
2. If you want the dressing to be thin, add a bit of almond milk. Allow the dressing to sit for a few minutes.
3. Chill the prepared dressing.

Notes:

- You can serve the dressing with any savory snacks, sandwiches, quick-bites, salads, etc.

- You can store the leftover dressing in the fridge for two days.

- You can add some ground nuts for enhancing the flavor.

PART III

Chapter 1: Introduction to the Heart-Healthy Diet

A heart-healthy diet is incredibly important. The truth is, you must be able to manage your diet well if you want to be healthy. The average diet is actually incredibly unhealthy for the heart, and the sooner that you are able to change up how you treat yourself and your body, the better off you will be. The average person consumes far too much salt and not enough of the important fruits and veggies that they need. As a result, they wind up with problems with their blood sugars, their blood pressure, and cholesterol levels. It is important to understand that your heart is one of the most important parts of your body—you cannot live without it. You need to keep it healthy. If you want to ensure that you can keep yourself healthy, you need to make sure that you eat the foods that will help you to nourish it readily. The sooner that you can do so, the better off you will be. This book is here to provide you with plenty of heart-healthy meals that you can enjoy that will help you to stay as healthy as possible.

The Rules of the Heart-Healthy Diet

Before we begin, let's go over some of the most important rules that go into the heart-healthy diet. These are rules that will help you to ensure that your body is kept as healthy as possible with foods that will nourish you well. Now, on this diet, you can expect to follow these rules:

1. **Decrease saturated and trans fats:** These are fats that are no good for anyone. Instead, it is recommended that you focus entirely on monounsaturated and polyunsaturated fats. These come from primarily vegetarian options—common sources include olive and canola oils, avocado, nuts, and fatty fish.

2. **Increase fruits and veggies:** Your body needs the vitamins and minerals in fruits and veggies to stay as healthy as possible. You should be consuming at least seven to nine servings per day to keep your body healthy and on track.

3. **Consume more fiber:** Typically, on this diet, you want to up your fiber intake. Fiber is necessary to keep your body regular. It also helps

with the way that you will naturally digest and absorb nutrients. You need both soluble and insoluble sources to stay as healthy as possible. Soluble fiber will aid in regulating your body and is fantastic for the heart. Insoluble fiber is there to help you regulate your weight and pass waste.

4. **Make the switch to plant proteins whenever possible:** You will also see that this diet advocates for more vegetarian options and less meat. While you can still eat meat, it is highly recommended that you choose to put in at least three servings of vegetable proteins, and you limit red meats down to just once a week. Twice a week, you should eat skinless poultry, and twice a week, you should enjoy fish.

5. **Up your whole grain intake:** This is essential to ensuring that you are not just consuming a bunch of empty carbs that aren't doing anything for you. By shifting to whole grains, you get more of the fiber that you need, and they are also usually full of better nutritional content as well.

6. **Limiting sweets:** If you are going to enjoy sweets, it is usually recommended that you cut out sugar or sugar-sweetened dishes. While you do not have to completely eliminate them, you should, at the very least, monitor and regulate intake.

7. **Low-fat dairy products:** You should have between two and three servings of dairy per day, but they ought to be reduced fat.

8. **Drink in moderation:** Alcohol is okay—but is not really encouraged either. If you must drink alcohol, make sure that you do so in moderation, which is typically defined as no more than one per day for women and no more than two per day for men.

The Benefits of the Heart-Healthy Diet

The heart-healthy diet has all sorts of benefits that are worth enjoying, and you should be able to treat these as motivation. If you find that you are struggling to enjoy this diet, consider these benefits to give you that added boost. Ultimately, the heart is the key to the body, and if you can keep it healthier, you will enjoy a better life for reasons such as:

- **Preventing heart disease:** When you limit salts, sweets, red meats, and everything else, you will help your heart remain healthier, and in doing so, you will reduce your risk of both stroke and heart disease.

- **Keeping your body healthier:** This diet is often recommended to older people, and this is for good reason—it keeps the body more agile by reducing the risk of frailty and muscle weakness.

- **Cutting the risk of Alzheimer's disease:** This diet helps your cholesterol, blood sugar, and blood vessel health, all of which are believed to aid in reducing the risk of both dementia and Alzheimer's disease.

- **Cutting the risk of Parkinson's disease:** Similarly, because this diet will be high in antioxidants, it has been found to cut the risk of Parkinson's disease significantly.

- **Longer lifespan:** This diet, because it lowers your risk of heart disease and cancer, is actually able to reduce your risk of death by around 20%.

- **Healthier mind:** If you suffer from anxiety or depression, this diet can actually help to alleviate some of the symptoms, or keep them at bay in the future. Between the healthy fats, rich vegetable content, and the boost to your gut bacteria, you will find that your body and mind both are healthier than ever.

- **It helps manage weight:** If you have struggled with your weight for some time, you may find that using this diet will actually help you to manage it, thanks to the fact that you'll be cutting out much of the foods that tend to lead to weight gain in the first place. You'll be able to enjoy a healthier body as the weight fades away through enjoying this diet.

Chapter 2: Heart-Healthy Savory Meals

Shrimp Scampi and Zoodles

Ingredients

- Butter (1 Tbsp., unsalted)
- Dry white wine (0.5 c.)
- Garlic (4 cloves, grated)
- Lemon juice (2 Tbsp.)
- Lemon zest (1 Tbsp.)
- Linguini (6 oz.)
- Olive oil (2 Tbsp.)
- Parsley (0.25 c., chopped)
- Red pepper flakes (0.25 tsp.)
- Shrimp (1.5 lbs., peeled and deveined—preferably large)
- Zucchini (3, spiralized)

Instructions

1. Start by preparing the pasta based on the instructions on the package. Keep 0.25 c. of the water to the side and drain the rest. Put pasta back in the pot.
2. Combine the shrimp, garlic, oil, salt, and pepper to taste and allow it to sit for five minutes.
3. Prepare a skillet and cook your shrimp in the garlicky oil over medium and garlic until done, roughly 3-4 minutes per side with a large count. Move shrimp to plate without the oil.
4. Add zest and pepper to the oil, along with the wine. Scrape the brown bits and reduce to 50%. Mix in lemon juice and butter, then toss the zoodles in.
5. After 2 minutes, add in shrimp, pasta, and combine well. Mix in water if necessary and toss with parsley.

Citrus Chicken Salad

Ingredients

- Baby kale (5 oz.)
- Chicken thighs (2 lbs.)
- Dijon mustard (1 tsp)
- Lemon juice (2 Tbsp.)
- Olive oil (2 Tbsp.)
- Orange (1, cut into 6 pieces)
- Salt and pepper
- Stale bread (8 oz., torn up into bite-sized bits)

Instructions

1. Warm oven to 425F. As it preheats, warm up half of your oil into a skillet. Then, salt and pepper the chicken, cooking it skin-side down in the oil. After 6 or 7 minutes, when the skin is golden, remove it to a baking sheet. Then, toss in the orange wedges and roast another 10 minutes until the chicken is completely cooked.
2. Reserve 2 Tbsp. of the chicken fat in the pot and then return it to low heat. Toss in the bread chunks, coating them in the fat. Add a quick sprinkle of salt and pepper, then cook until toasted, usually about 8 minutes or so. Set aside.
3. Warm pan on medium-low, then toss in lemon juice. Deglaze the pan for a minute, then remove from heat. Combine with Dijon mustard and juice from roasted oranges. Mix in remaining oil.
4. Add kale and croutons to skillet to mix well, coating it in the mixture. Serve immediately with chicken.

Shrimp Taco Salad

Ingredients

- 3 Fresh lime juice (3 tbsp.)
- Avocado (1)
- Cayenne pepper sauce (1 tsp.)
- Cilantro leaves (1 c.)
- Corn chips (such as Fritos-- 2 c.)
- Extra-virgin olive oil (0.25 c.)
- Fresh corn (3 pieces)
- Ground coriander (0.25 tsp.)
- Ground cumin (0.25 tsp.)
- Salt
- Shrimp (1 lb.)
- Watermelon (2 c.)
- Zucchini (2 medium)

Instructions

1. Set up your grill to medium heat.
2. First grill the corn until it begins to char, usually about 10 minutes, with the occasional turn. At the same time, allow zucchini to grill for around 6 minutes until beginning to soften. Shrimp requires 2-4 minutes until cooked through, flipping once.
3. Combine your oil, juice, and seasonings, with just a pinch of salt.
4. Remove the kernels off of your corn and slice up your zucchini. Place zucchini and avocado onto a plate, topping it with the corn, then the watermelon, and finally the shrimp. You can leave it as is until you're ready to eat—it keeps for about a day in the fridge.
5. To serve, top with the chips (crumbled) and the dressing mix.

Chicken, Green Bean, Bacon Pasta

Ingredients

- Bacon (4 slices)
- Chicken breast (1 lb., cut into bite-sized bits)
- Egg yolk (1 large)
- Green beans (fresh—8 oz., trimmed and cut in half)
- Half-and-half (2 Tbsp.)
- Lemon juice (2 Tbsp.)
- Parmesan cheese (1 oz., grated—about 0.5 c.)
- Penne pasta (12 oz.)
- Scallions (2, sliced thinly)
- Spinach (5 oz.)

Instructions

1. Prepare pasta according to the package. Then, at the last minute of cooking, toss in the beans. Drain, reserving 0.5 c. of the cooking water. Leave pasta mix in the pot.
2. In a skillet, start preparing the bacon until crisp. Dry on a paper towel and then break into bits when cooled. Clean pan, reserving 1 Tbsp. of bacon fat.
3. On medium heat, cook the chicken until browning and cooked all the way. Then, off of the burner, toss in the lemon juice.
4. Mix together your egg and half-and-half in a separate container. Then, dump it to coat in the pasta and green beans, then toss in the chicken, spinach, and cheese. Mix well to coat. Add pasta water if needed, 0.25 c. at a time. Mix in the scallions, then top with bacon. Serve.

Heart-Healthy "Fried" Chicken

Ingredients

- Blackening seasoning (2 tsp.)
- Buttermilk (0.5 c.)
- Chicken drumsticks (2 lb., skinless)
- Cornflakes (4 c.)
- Olive oil (1 Tbsp.)
- Parsley (0.5 c., chopped)
- Salt (a pinch to taste)

Instructions

1. Get ready to bake the chicken at a temperature of 375F and make sure that you've got something to bake on that is currently protected.
2. Mix buttermilk, seasoning, and a touch of salt.
3. Crush cornflakes and put them in a second bowl. Combine with the oil and parsley.
4. Prep chicken by dipping first in buttermilk, letting it drip, then coating in cornflakes. Bake for 30-35 minutes.

Turkey Burgers and Slaw

Ingredients

Slaw

- Apple (1, matchstick-cut)
- Cabbage (8 oz., thinly sliced)
- Honey (1 Tbsp.)
- Jalapeno (1, thinly sliced and seeded)
- Lime juice (3 Tbsp.)
- Red wine vinegar (1 Tbsp.)
- Salt and pepper, to your preference

Burgers

- Buns (4, toasted lightly)
- Chili paste (1.5 Tbsp.)

- Ginger (1 Tbsp., grated)
- Olive oil (2 Tbsp.)
- Onion (0.5 chopped)
- Soy sauce (1 Tbsp.)
- Turkey (1 lb., ground up)

Instructions

1. Mix together the liquids for the slaw and the seasoning. Mix well, then toss in the slaw ingredients. Set aside.
2. Prepare your burger mixture, adding everything together, but the oil and the buns somewhere that you can mix them up. Combine well, then form four patties.
3. Prepare to your preference. Grills work well, or you choose to, you could use a cast iron pan with the oil. Cook until done.
4. Serve on buns with slaw and any other condiments you may want.

Slow Cooked Shrimp and Pasta
Ingredients

- Acini di pepe (4 oz., cooked to package specifications)
- Basil (0.25 c., chopped fresh)
- Diced tomatoes (14.5 oz. can)
- Feta (2 oz., crumbled)
- Garlic (2 cloves, minced)
- Kalamata olives (8, chopped)
- Olive oil (1 Tbsp.)
- Pinch of salt
- Rosemary (1.5 tsp fresh, chopped)
- Shrimp (8 oz., fresh or frozen)
- Sweet red bell pepper (1, chopped)
- White wine (0.5 c.) or chicken broth (o.5 c.)
- Zucchini (1 c., sliced)

Instructions

1. Thaw, peel, and devein shrimp. Set aside in fridge until ready to use them.
2. Coat your slow cooker insert with cooking spray, then add in tomato, zucchini tomatoes, bell pepper, and garlic.
3. Cook on low for 4 hours, or high for 2 hours. Mix in shrimp. Then, keep heat on high. Cook covered for 30 minutes.
4. Prepare pasta according to the instructions on the packaging.
5. Mix in the olives, rosemary, basil, oil, and salt.
6. Serve with pasta topped with shrimp, then topped with feta.

Chapter 3: Heart-Healthy Sweet Treats

Chocolate Mousse

Ingredients

- Avocado (1 large, pitted and skinned)
- Cocoa powder (2 Tbsp., unsweetened)
- Nondairy milk of choice (3 Tbsp., unsweetened)
- Nonfat vanilla Greek yogurt (0.25 c.)
- Semi-sweet baking chocolate (2 oz., melted and cooling)
- Sweetener packet if desired.
- Vanilla extract (1 tsp.)

Instructions

1. Prepare by putting all ingredients but sugar into a food processor. Combine well. Taste. If you want it sweeter, add in some sweetener as well.

2. Chill in your fridge until you are ready to serve.

Baked Pears
Ingredients

- Almonds (0.25 c., chopped)
- Brown sugar (0.33 c., can sub with honey)
- Butter (2 oz., melted, or coconut oil if you prefer vegan)
- Ground cinnamon (1 tsp)
- Ripe pears (3)
- Rolled oats (0.5 c.)
- Salt (a pinch)
- Sugar (pinch)

Instructions

1. Set oven to 400 F.
2. Incorporate all dry ingredients. Then, mix half of your melted butter.
3. Cut your pears in half and carve out the cores, making a nice scoop in the center. Brush with butter, then top with a sprinkle of sugar.
4. Put your cinnamon oat mixture into the centers of the pears.
5. Bake for 30-40 minutes, until soft.

Chocolate Peanut Butter Bites

Ingredients

- Chocolate chips of choice (2 c.)
- Coconut flour (1 c.)
- Honey (0.75 c.)
- Smooth peanut butter (2 c.)

Instructions

1. Prepare a tray with parchment paper to avoid sticking or messes
2. Melt together your peanut butter and honey, mixing well
3. Add coconut flour to peanut butter mixture and combine to incorporate. If it's still thin, add small amounts of flour. Let it thicken for 10 minutes.
4. Create 20 balls out of the dough.
5. Melt chocolate, then dip the dough balls into the chocolate and place them on the parchment. Refrigerate until firm.

Oatmeal Cookies

Ingredients

- Applesauce (2.5 Tbsp.)
- Baking soda (0.25 tsp)
- Coconut oil (2 Tbsp., melted)
- Dark chocolate chips (0.25 c.)
- Honey (0.25 c.)
- Salt (0.5 tsp)
- Vanilla extract (2 tsp.)
- Whole grain oats (0.5 c.)
- Whole wheat flour (0.5 c.)

Instructions

1. Set your oven to 350 F.
2. Mix syrup, oil (melted), applesauce, and vanilla.
3. Toss in salt, baking soda, oats, and flour. Combine well until it becomes a dough.
4. Mix the chocolate chips in.
5. Put in tablespoons onto cookie sheet.
6. Bake for 10 minutes. Let cool before transferring to a cooling rack.

Pina Colada Frozen Dessert

Ingredients

- Butter (0.25 c.)
- Crushed pineapple in juice (undrained—1 8 oz. can)
- Graham cracker crumbs (1.25 c.)
- Rum extract or rum (0.25 c.)
- Sugar (1 Tbsp.)
- Toasted flaked coconut (0.25 c.)
- Vanilla low-fat, no-sugar ice cream (4 c.)

Instructions

1. Prepare oven to 350 F.
2. Combine butter, cracker crumbs, and sugar. Press into a 2-quart baking dish. Bake 10 minutes and allow to cool completely
3. Combine ice cream, pineapple and juice, and extracts into a bowl with a mixer until well combined. Spread it out into the crust.
4. Freeze for 6 hours.
5. Serve after letting thaw for 5 minutes and topping with coconut shreds.

Kiwi Sorbet

Ingredients

- Kiwi (1 lb., peeled and frozen)
- Honey (0.25 c.)

Instructions

1. Combine everything well in a food processor until mixed.
2. Pour it into a loaf pan and smooth it out.
3. Allow it to freeze for 2 hours. Keep it covered if leaving it overnight in the freezer.

Ricotta Brûlée

Ingredients

- Ricotta cheese (2 c.)
- Lemon zest (1 tsp)
- Honey (2 Tbsp.)
- Sugar (2 Tbsp.)

Instructions

1. Mix together your ricotta, lemon zest, and honey. Then, split into ramekins. Top with sugar and place onto baking sheet.
2. Place oven rack at the topmost position then set the baking sheet in with the broiler on its highest setting. Watch closely and broil until it bubbles and turns golden brown—between 5 and 10 minutes.
3. Cool for 10 minutes and top with any fruits or toppings you prefer.

Chapter 4: Heart-Healthy Gourmet Meals

Grilled Halibut With Pine Nut Relish
Ingredients

- Diced red tomato (0.5 c.)
- Diced yellow tomato (0.5 c)
- EVOO (3 Tbsp.)
- Flour to coat fish
- Green olives (0.5 c.)
- Halibut fillet (4, 1 inch thick)
- Kalamata olives (0.5 c.)
- Lemon juice (1 Tbsp.)
- Zest from a lemon (0.5 tsp.)
- Parsley (2 Tbsp.)
- Pepper to taste
- Pine nuts (3 Tbsp.)
- Salt (pinch to taste)
- Shallot (1)

Instructions

1. Start with toasting the pine nuts in a dry skillet for a few minutes until toasted. Set aside.
2. Combine your tomatoes, the sliced olives, shallot, the lemon juice and zest, and 1 Tbsp. of oil. Mix well and add in parsley and a sprinkle of pepper.
3. Flour fillets, shaking off excess. Season lightly with salt and pepper. Toss the rest of your oil into your skillet and use that to cook the fish until done, flipping halfway over.
4. Serve with relish on top and garnish with pine nuts.

Shrimp Bowls

Ingredients

- Avocado (1, cut small)
- Broccoli (1 lb., florets)
- Ginger (1 Tbsp.)
- Olive oil (2 Tbsp.)
- Plum tomatoes (8 oz., seeds removed and cut)
- Quinoa (1.5 c.)
- Rice vinegar (1 Tbsp.)
- Salt and pepper to taste
- Scallions (2, thinly sliced)
- Shrimp (20 large, peeled and deveined)

Instructions

1. Warm oven to 425 F. Prepare medium saucepan at medium heat and cook the quinoa until toasted, roughly 5 minutes. Add in water (3 c.), then cover immediately. Allow it to cook just below a boil for 10 minutes, then take it off the burner and let it sit for another ten minutes.
2. On a baking sheet, add broccoli, 1 Tbsp. oil, salt, and pepper. Prepare in a single layer. Roast for 15 minutes. Season shrimp, then cook for 6-8 minutes, tossed with broccoli.
3. Mix vinegar, ginger, and remaining oil into a small bowl. Toss with tomatoes and scallions.
4. Serve with quinoa in bowls, topped with broccoli shrimp, then avocado. Finally, add the vinaigrette to the top.

Grilled Watermelon Steak Salad

Ingredients

- Cherry tomatoes (1 lb., halved)
- Honey (1 tsp)
- Lemon juice (3 Tbsp.)
- Mint leaves (1 c., torn up)
- Olive oil (2 Tbsp.)
- Onion (0.5 tsp., small red)
- Parsley (1 c., chopped)
- Salt and pepper
- Sirloin steak (1 lb.)
- Unsalted peanuts to garnish
- Watermelon (3 lbs., seedless)

Instructions

1. Prepare grill to medium-high. Season steak, then grill until done to preference. Allow it to rest on a cutting board.
2. Mix oil, lemon juice, honey, and seasonings. Incorporate the onions and tomatoes as well, folding in nicely.
3. Cut watermelon into 0.5-inch thick triangles and remove rinds. Oil and grill until starting to char—a minute per side, then set aside.
4. Mix the herbs into the tomato mixture. Serve with watermelon topped with stead.

Crispy Cod and Green Beans

Ingredients

- Green Beans (1 lb.)
- Olive oil (2 Tbsp.)
- Parmesan cheese (0.25 c., grated)
- Pepper to taste
- Pesto (2 Tbsp.)
- Salt to taste
- Skinless cod (1.25 lb., four pieces)

Instructions

1. Set oven to 425 F. Put beans onto rimmed baking sheet and combine with 1 Tbsp. oil, then top with cheese and a sprinkling of seasonings. Roast for 10-12 minutes, waiting for it to finally start to brown.
2. Heat remaining oil in a skillet. Season cod and cook until golden brown. You want to use a medium-high heat to do this.
3. Serve with pesto over cod, next to a bed of green beans.

Pistachio-Crusted Fish

Ingredients

- Baby spinach (4 c.)
- Greek yogurt (4 Tbsp.)
- Lemon juice (2 Tbsp.)
- Olive oil (2 Tbsp.)
- Panko (whole-wheat, 0.25 c.)
- Pepper (0.5 tsp)
- Quinoa (0.75 c.)
- Salt (0.75 tsp)
- Shelled pistachios, chopped (0.25 c.)
- Tilapia (4 6-oz. pieces)

Instructions

1. Prepare quinoa based on instructions on packaging.
2. Season fish with salt, pepper, and coat with 1 Tbsp. each of Greek yogurt.
3. Combine panko and pistachios, tossing with 1 Tbsp. olive oil. Gently sprinkle over the top of the fish, pressing it to stick. Bake for 12 minutes at 375 F., or until done.
4. Combine cooked quinoa with spinach, lemon juice, remaining oil, and a pinch of salt and pepper. Serve with fish.

Cumin-Spiced Lamb and Salad

Ingredients

- Carrots (1 lb.)
- Cumin (1.25 tsp.)
- Honey (0.5 tsp.)
- Lamb loin chops (8—about 2 lbs.)
- Mint leaves (0.25 c., fresh)
- Olive oil (3 Tbsp.)
- Radishes (6)
- Red wine vinegar (2 Tbsp.)
- Salt and pepper to taste

Instructions

1. Combine 2 Tbsp. oil, vinegar, a pinch of cumin, honey, and salt and pepper.
2. Warm remaining oil in a skillet at medium. Season lamb with cumin and a pinch of salt and pepper. Cook until preferred doneness.
3. Shave carrots into pieces and create thinly sliced radishes. Coat with dressing and mix with mint. Serve with lamb.

Chapter 5: Heart-Healthy Quick 'n Easy Meals

Sugar Snap Pea and Radish Salad

Ingredients

- Apple-cider vinegar (2 Tbsp.)

- Avocado (0.5, medium ripe)
- Dijon mustard (0.5 tsp)
- Fresh lemon juice (1 Tbsp.)
- Freshly ground pepper (0.5 tsp)
- Ground coriander (0.25 tsp)
- Olive oil (0.25 c.)
- Radishes (12, small)
- Salt (o.5 tsp)
- Sugar snap peas (1 lb.)
- Watermelon radish (1, small)

Instructions

1. Combine peas and radishes in a bowl together.
2. In a blender, combine everything else and puree until well combined and smooth. Add water if necessary to thin it out.
3. Coat radish and peas with dressing and serve.

Horseradish Salmon Cakes

Ingredients

- Dijon mustard (1 Tbsp.)
- English cucumber (1, small)
- Greek Yogurt (2 Tbsp.)
- Horseradish (2 Tbsp.)
- Lemon juice (1 Tbsp.)
- Olive oil (2 Tbsp.)
- Panko (0.25 c.)
- Salt and pepper to taste
- Skinless salmon filet (1.25 lb.)
- Watercress (1 bunch)

Instructions

1. Combine salmon, horseradish, salt and pepper, and mustard into a food processor until well chopped. Then, toss in the bread crumbs and combine well.
2. Form 8 patties.
3. Warm 1 Tbsp. oil in a skillet. Cook until opaque throughout, typically 2 minutes before flipping.
4. Combine yogurt, lemon juice, oil, and a sprinkle of salt and pepper. Combine in cucumber slices, then watercress.
5. Serve salmon with salad.

Salmon, Green Beans, and Tomatoes

Ingredients

- Garlic (6 cloves)
- Green beans (1 lb.)
- Grape tomatoes (1 pint)
- Kalamata olives (0.5 c.)
- Anchovy fillets (3)
- Olive oil (2 Tbsp.)
- Kosher salt and pepper to personal preference
- Salmon fillet, skinless

Instructions

1. Prepare oven to 425 F. Put beans, garlic, olive, anchovy, and tomatoes together along with half of the oil and a pinch of pepper. Roast until veggies are tender.
2. Warm the remainder of the oil over a skillet at medium heat. Season salmon, then cook until done. Serve salmon and veggies together.

Broccoli Pesto Fusilli
Ingredients

- Basil leaves (0.5 c.)

- Broccoli florets (12 oz.)
- Fusilli (12 oz.)
- Garlic (2 cloves)
- Lemon zest (1 Tbsp.)
- Olive oil (3 Tbsp.)
- Parmesan cheese to garnish
- Salt to taste
- Sliced almonds to garnish

Instructions

1. Prepare pasta to directions and reserve 0.5 c. of the liquid.
2. Combine broccoli, garlic, and the reserved water in a bowl and cook for five or six minutes, stirring halfway through. Put everything right into a food processor with the liquid. Combine in basil, oil, zest, a pinch of salt, and puree.
3. Put pasta in with pesto. Drizzle in water if necessary. Sprinkle with cheese and nuts if desired. Serve immediately.

Strawberry Spinach Salad

Ingredients

- Baby spinach (3 c.)
- Medium avocado (0.25, diced)
- Red onion (1 Tbsp.)
- Sliced strawberries (0.5 c.)
- Vinaigrette of choice (2 Tbsp.)
- Walnut pieces (roasted)

Instructions

1. Combine spinach with the berries and onion. Mix well. Coat with vinaigrette and toss. Then, top with walnuts and avocado. Serve.

One-Pot Shrimp and Spinach

Ingredients

- Crushed red pepper (0.25 tsp)
- Garlic (6 cloves, sliced)
- Lemon juice (1 Tbsp.)
- Lemon zest (1.5 tsp.)
- Olive oil (3 Tbsp.)
- Parsley (1 Tbsp.)
- Salt to personal preference
- Shrimp (1 lb.)
- Spinach (1 lb.)

Instructions

1. Warm skillet with 1 Tbsp. oil. Cook half of the garlic until browning, about a single minute. Then, toss in spinach and salt. Wait for it to wilt over the heat, about 5 minutes. Remove and mix in lemon juice, storing it in a separate bowl.
2. Warm heat to medium-high and toss with remainder of oil. Toss in the rest of your garlic and cook until browning. Then, mix in shrimp, pepper, and salt. Cook until shrimp is done, then serve atop spinach with lemon zest and parsley garnish.

Chapter 6: Heart-Healthy Vegetarian and Vegan Meals

Vegetarian Butternut Squash Torte

Ingredients

- Butternut squash (1 lb.)
- Crusty bread of choice
- Kale (1, small)
- Olive oil (1 Tbsp.)
- Parmesan cheese (4 Tbsp., grated)
- Plum tomato (1)
- Provolone cheese (6 oz., thinly sliced)
- Red onion (1, medium)
- Salt and pepper to taste
- Yukon Gold potato (1, medium)

Instructions

1. Take a spring form 9-inch pan and prepare it so that nothing will stick. Then, take your squash and put it around the bottom in circles to sort of mimic a crust.
2. Then, layer it with the onion, with the rings separated out.
3. Add half of your kale, then sprinkle half of your oil, and season to taste.
4. Then, layer with potatoes, half of your cheese, and top with the last of your kale.
5. Add the oil, onion, tomato slices, and the last of your cheese.
6. Top it with the remainder of your squash, then coat with parmesan.
7. Bake, covering the top with foil, for 20 minutes. Then, discard the foil and let it bake until it is tender and browning, typically another ten minutes or so.

Vegetarian Fried Rice

Ingredients

- 2 eggs (leave out if vegan)
- Garlic (2 cloves, pressed)
- Kale (6 oz., thinly sliced leaves)
- Olive oil (1 Tbsp.)
- Rice (4 c., cooked and chilled, preferably the day before)
- Sesame oil (1 Tbsp.)
- Shiitake mushroom caps (4 oz., sliced)
- Soy sauce (2 Tbsp., low sodium)
- Sriracha (1 tsp.)

Instructions

1. Start by warming your oil up in your pan of choice or wok. Your oil should be just before the smoking point.
2. Cook the mushrooms and toss until they start to turn golden brown, usually just a few minutes, then set them off for later.
3. Toss in some sesame oil and kale, cooking until wilted, then add in your garlic as well for another minute.
4. Take your rice and mix it in as well, tossing it together until heated.
5. Move all rice to the side, then pour beaten eggs in the center of your pan. Stir often until the eggs are just about finished, and then mix into the rice.
6. Mix in the soy sauce and sriracha, then top with mushrooms.

Vegan Butternut Squash Soup

Ingredients

- Butternut squash (1, 2.5 lbs. with skin and seeds removed—keep seeds)
- Carrots (2 medium, cut into 1-inch pieces)
- Coconut milk (2 Tbsp.)
- Olive oil (2 Tbsp., and one tsp)
- Onion (1, large, chopped)
- Pepper (2.25 tsp)
- Turmeric (2.25 tsp)
- Veggie bouillon base (1 Tbsp.)

Instructions

1. Take a Dutch oven and add 2 Tbsp. oil. Warm, then cook your onions until soft and translucent, roughly 6 minutes or so.
2. Integrate your bouillon base with 6 c., boiling water until completely dissolved.
3. Toss together your veggies, turmeric, and pepper into your onions in the Dutch oven. Allow it to cook for a minute before mixing in your veggie broth. Simmer for 20 minutes until veggies are soft.
4. Turn your oven to 375F. Take your seeds and your oil that is remaining and combine them together. Then, coat it up with the turmeric and pepper before toasting in your oven for about 1o minutes.
5. With a blender or immersion blender, combine your soup until smooth.
6. Serve topped with seeds and a swirl of coconut milk.

Vegetarian Kale and Sweet Potato Frittata

Ingredients

- Eggs (6)
- Garlic (2 cloves)
- Goat cheese (3 oz.)
- Half-and-half (1 c.)
- Kale (2 c., packed tightly)
- Olive oil (2 Tbsp.)
- Pepper (0.5 tsp.)
- Red onion (0.5, small)
- Salt (1 tsp.)
- Sweet potatoes (2 c.)

Instructions

1. With your oven warming, combine your eggs in a bowl. Then, add in the salt and half-and-half as well. Make sure your oven is at 350F.

2. In a nonstick skillet that you can put into your oven, cook your potatoes over 1 Tbsp. of oil. Wait for them to soften and start to turn golden. Then, remove from the pan.
3. Next, cook your kale, onion, and garlic together in the remainder of your oil until it is wilted and aromatic.
4. Put your potato back in with the kale, then pour your egg mix atop it all. Incorporate well and then allow it to cook on the stove for another 3 minutes.
5. Top it all with the goat cheese, then bake for 10 minutes until completely done.

Vegan Ginger Ramen

Ingredients

- Garlic (4 cloves, minced)
- Ginger (0.33 c., chopped coarsely)
- Grapeseed oil (0.5 c.)
- Low-sodium soy sauce (2 Tbsp.)
- Pepper (1 tsp., freshly ground)
- Ramen noodles (*real*, fresh noodles—not the $0.10 packaged stuff)
- Rice vinegar (1 Tbsp.)
- Salt to personal preference
- Scallions (1 bunch—about 2 c. sliced)
- Sesame oil (1 tsp)
- Sugar (0.5 tsp)

Instructions

1. Combine your ginger with the minced garlic and roughly 60% of your scallions.
2. Warm up the grapeseed oil until just before the smoking point. Then, take the oil and dump it over your scallion mix. It will sizzle and wilt, turning green. Leave it for 5 minutes, then add in the rest of the scallions.
3. Carefully combine in soy sauce, sesame oil, vinegar, sugar, and pepper, and leave it to incorporate for the next 15 minutes or so. Adjust flavor accordingly.
4. Prepare your noodles to the package instructions. Drain.
5. Introduce your noodles to your scallion sauce and coat well.
6. Serve topped with sesame seeds or any other toppings you may want.

Vegan Glazed Tofu

Ingredients

- Canola oil (0.5 c.)
- Firm tofu (12 oz.)
- Ginger (0.5" sliced thinly)
- Maple syrup (3 Tbsp.—you can use honey if you're not vegan.)
- Pepper flakes (0.5 tsp.)
- Rice vinegar (3 Tbsp.)
- Soy sauce (4 Tbsp.)
- Toppings of choice—recommended ones include rice, scallions, or sesame seeds

Instructions

1. Dry and drain your tofu out, squeezing it between paper towels so that you can remove as much of the liquid as you possibly can, then slice it into cubes.
2. Combine the wet ingredients together, and add in your pepper and ginger.
3. Warm your wok or skillet. When the oil is shimmery, gingerly place your tofu into it carefully and leave it for around 4 minutes so that it can brown. It should be dark brown when you flip. Repeat on both sides. Then, drop the heat down and toss in your sauce mix. Allow it to reduce until it is thick, roughly 4 minutes.
4. Put tofu on plates and top with anything you desire.

Vegan Greek Tofu Breakfast Scramble

Ingredients

- Basil (0.25 c., chopped)
- Firm tofu block (8 oz.)
- Garlic (2 cloves, diced)
- Grape tomatoes (0.5 c., halved)
- Kalamata olives (0.25 c., halved)
- Lemon juice (from ½ lemon)
- Nutritional yeast (2 Tbsp.)
- Olive oil (1 Tbsp.)
- Red bell pepper (0.5 c., chopped)
- Red onion (0.25, diced)
- Salt (pinch)
- Spinach (1 handful)
- Tahini paste (1 tsp)
- Salt and pepper to personal preference

Instructions

1. Break down tofu until the shape/texture of scrambled eggs. Then, combine in yeast, lemon juice, and tahini. Sprinkle with a pinch of salt.
2. Prepare skillet at a moderate heat. Sauté onions for 5 minutes before tossing in the pepper and garlic for an additional 5 minutes.
3. Mix in tofu and Kalamata olives. Warm through.
4. Toss in greens until wilted and reduced. Take off from heat and toss in tomatoes and season with salt and pepper to taste.

www.ingramcontent.com/pod-product-compliance
Lightning Source LLC
LaVergne TN
LVHW020418070526
838199LV00055B/3654